D1605854

Everyday Project Management

Jeff Davidson

BK

Berrett-Koehler Publishers, Inc.

Berrett-Koehler Publishers, Inc.
1333 Broadway, Suite 1000
Oakland, CA 94612-1921
Tel: (510) 817-2277
Fax: (510) 817-2278
www.bkconnection.com

ORDERING INFORMATION
Quantity sales. Special discounts are available on quantity purchases by corporations, associations, and others. For details, contact the "Special Sales Department" at the Berrett-Koehler address above.

Individual sales. Berrett-Koehler publications are available through most bookstores. They can also be ordered directly from Berrett-Koehler:
Tel: (800) 929-2929; Fax: (802) 864-7626; www.bkconnection.com.

Orders for college textbook / course adoption use. Please contact Berrett-Koehler:
Tel: (800) 929-2929; Fax: (802) 864-7626.

Distributed to the U.S. trade and internationally by Penguin Random House Publisher Services.

Berrett-Koehler and the BK logo are registered trademarks of Berrett-Koehler Publishers, Inc.

Printed in the United States of America

Berrett-Koehler books are printed on long-lasting, acid-free paper. When it is available, we choose paper that has been manufactured by environmentally responsible processes. These may include using trees grown in sustainable forests, incorporating recycled paper, minimizing chlorine in bleaching, or recycling the energy produced at the paper mill.

Library of Congress Cataloging-in-Publication Data
Names: Davidson, Jeffrey P., author.
Title: Everyday project management / Jeff Davidson.
Description: First edition. | Oakland, CA : Berrett-Koehler Publishers, [2019] |
   Includes bibliographical references and index.
Identifiers: LCCN 2019009583 | ISBN 9781523085392 (pbk. : alk paper)
Subjects: LCSH: Project management.
Classification: LCC HD69.P75 D3792 2019 | DDC 658.4/04—dc23
LC record available at https://lccn.loc.gov/2019009583

First Edition
29 28 27 26 25 24 23 22 21 20 19   10 9 8 7 6 5 4 3 2 1

Book producer Westchester Publishing Services
Cover production: Dan Tesser, Studio Carnelian

*This book is dedicated to the project managers
across America and around the globe—
the men and women who work with teams in the
trenches, who report to sponsors and shareholders
of all types, and who ultimately complete the
projects of the world, so that everyone can
benefit from the results of their efforts.*

Contents

Contents at a Glance

Chapter 1: Project Management in a World of Overload
Learn why having work-life balance is vital to project managers who seek long and prosperous careers, and discover the importance of learning project management basics.

Chapter 2: Industry Norms—Should You Conform?
Learn why it's worthwhile to gain a rudimentary understanding of project management before enrolling in a tech-savvy program or course of study bolstered by software and prevailing project management terminology.

Chapter 3: So, You're Going to Manage a Project?
Learn what a project is, essential skills for project managers, and what it takes to be a good project manager.

Chapter 4: What Makes a Good Project Manager?
Learn the traits of successful project managers, the reasons that project managers succeed, and the reasons that they fail.

Chapter 5: What Do You Want to Accomplish?
Learn the importance of fully understanding the project, what kinds of projects lend themselves to project management, and why it's vital to start with the end in mind.

Chapter 6: Laying Out Your Plan

Learn the guiding principle of project managers, all about plotting your course, initiating a work breakdown structure, and the difference between action and results (deliverables).

Chapter 7: Assembling Your Plan

Learn how to further refine your work breakdown structure (WBS), whether your labor should be part of the WBS, the importance of reintegrating project staff as the project winds down, and distinctions between the WBS and other planning tools.

Chapter 8: Keeping Your Eye on the Budget

Learn effective approaches to budgeting, how to combine top-down and bottom-up budgeting techniques, how optimism stands in the way of controlling expenses, and the importance of building in slack.

Chapter 9: Gantt Charts

Learn what a Gantt chart is, why it's valuable in project management, how Gantt charts keep your project on schedule, and variations that you can devise.

Chapter 10: Critical Path Method

Learn why projects become increasingly complex, the basics of the critical path method (CPM), and how to use the critical path method to conserve resources.

Chapter 11: Choosing Project Management Software

Learn the kinds of software that are available, the capabilities of software, which software functions are crucial, and guidelines for selection.

Chapter 12: A Sampling of Popular Programs

Learn which software programs are popular, what vendors have to say about their own programs, and the importance of taking your time when acquiring software.

Chapter 13: Reporting Results

Learn about potential difficulties in reporting your results, how to effectively use communication tools and techniques, the value of giving credit to your team, and the importance of assuming any blame alone.

Chapter 14: Multiple Bosses and Multiple Projects, and Staying Balanced

Learn how to keep your wits on multiple projects, help your bosses not to overload you, handle multiple reporting structures, and be assertive when overload seems unavoidable.

Chapter 15: Real-World Project Management Results

Learn why a thorough initial research phase can pay off handsomely for your project, the difference between squeaking by and excelling, and why open and easy communication is critical to your project's success.

Chapter 16: Learning from Your Experience

Learn how to maintain perspective in your role as project manager, the enduring value of mastering project management software, why it pays to keep your eyes and ears open, and how to be ready for what's next.

Preface

Suppose you're a rising star at work and the boss has given you your first assignment to head up a project. Depending on the nature of the project and what kind of work you do, you might have to engage in a variety of tasks that you haven't tackled before, such as assembling a team to complete the project on time and on budget, mapping out a plan and monitoring your progress at key steps along the way, using appropriate planning tools such as project management software or wall charts, and keeping your team motivated and on target.

Perhaps you have managed projects before, but not recently. Or, you have been given a new kind of project with which you're not familiar, and you want to ensure that you handle the job correctly. If so, you've come to the right place. *Everyday Project Management* provides you with the essence of what you need to know, in terms of successful project management.

Each chapter can be read and absorbed in about 20 minutes. The book covers vital aspects of project management, including plotting your path, drawing on age-old as well as current supporting tools, assembling a winning team, expending your resources wisely, monitoring your progress, adjusting course when needed, and learning from your experience so you will be even better at managing projects in the future.

If you're like many professionals today, you are busy! Your time is precious. When you're handed a challenging assignment and need some direction, you need it in a hurry. And that is what *Everyday Project Management* offers you: guidance in the form of a quick reference tool—divided into 16 crucial aspects of project management—that cover the basics. You'll be able to complete a chapter each morning if you choose, before everyone else arrives at work. Also, key glossary terms are provided, along with a list of further reading. So, with this handy guide, you're not more than a few pages away from homing in on the information you require.

No Need for Dread

If you're unfamiliar with project management, or it has been a while since you've managed a project, fear not. Project management can be a rewarding, even exhilarating experience. Yet, many people head into it feeling a mild streak of terror, if not outright dread. Why so? Because the levels of sophistication one can bring to the role of project management vary wildly, and it's easy to get confused or feel overwhelmed.

The largest of projects, such as launching a space capsule, developing a gene therapy process, or building an intercontinental shipping fleet, can require months of work, if not years or decades, and can involve several hundred to several thousand people, with a budget that ranges well into the multimillions of dollars. If that is the kind of project you'll be tackling, you need a different book!

Everyday Project Management explains the role of the project manager in the conception, planning, execution, control, and completion of a project. It is designed for project managers in all types of settings, but particularly for the career professional who's been assigned to manage a project, alone or with a staff of, say, 10 or fewer people. The project is likely to last for a few months or less and to cost less than $1 million. Still, you need to know about effective project management—and probably quickly.

Each of the 16 chapters provides essential nuggets of wisdom that will carry you along with an understanding of what your role as project manager involves, the kinds of challenges you'll encounter, the interpersonal issues that will arise, and how to stay on time and on budget in pursuit of the desired, quality outcome.

Everyday Project Management offers instruction in bite-size segments, while recognizing that you're not frantically studying to obtain a Project Management Institute (PMI) certificate. Still, you seek to know the fundamentals of project management; to be able to discuss them, perhaps, with certified professionals; and to indicate that you are, indeed, in the game.

This Book Is for You

While the topic of project management could seem somewhat dry on the surface, *Everyday Project Management* will surely hold your attention. Unlike other books on project management, here I'll underscore the importance of balance and pacing oneself, as well as incorporating the fundamentals. I'll keep the text relatively jargon free and will explain vital terms.

As your author, while I had no formal training in project management, I have an MBA from the University of Connecticut, and years ago earned the certified management consultant (CMC) designation awarded by the Institute of

Management Consultants. The approach I take in writing this book is to draw on classic texts from established authors in the field of project management and to incorporate the vital input of three veteran project managers who lead major projects within their respective organizations—added to my years of hands-on experience in managing consulting projects, with a staff of anywhere from two to 10 people, ranging from weeks to many months in duration, and with budgets from a few thousand dollars to as much as $490,000.

Beyond this book, a variety of supporting tools at your disposal can help steer you to a successful end. These include everything from planning guides, to wall charts, to a sophisticated array of software tools—the initial portions of which you can learn within a day and be up and running by the second day. *Everyday Project Management* will introduce you to such tools so that you have a good grasp of their benefits.

The great news is that if you are a fairly organized person and have already accomplished notable deeds, you likely have excellent potential for being an effective project manager. Once you've successfully completed your first project, or your first project in a while, you might find that you're ready to tackle the next, and the next. That will boost your career, because managing projects gives you visibility and exposure within your organization that you might not otherwise muster.

Introduction

Independent of what college you attended (if you went to one), what you studied, where you first worked, your current organization, how long you've been in project management, the size of your budget, the number of people on your staff, and so forth, it's likely that you fall into one of three groups of people who are attracted to learning about *Everyday Project Management*. Where do *you* fit?

1. Newbies

This group consists of people who are new to project management and probably not familiar with the basic concepts. They lack on-the-job experience; thus, they need to gear up quickly. Perhaps they come from an engineering discipline or the military. First-time project managers tend to be younger, but not necessarily!

If from engineering, your expertise could be in physical projects such as civil, mechanical, or structural engineering, or even in software engineering. Engineers often are good at implementing plans, but eventually they seek to coordinate larger projects, not simply dwell on their own tasks. Maybe you bought *Everyday Project Management* because you view project management as a stepping stone in your overall career progression.

Coming from an engineering background, you might not have had opportunities to hone your social and interpersonal skills. It sounds stereotypical, but you might be effective with quantitative tools yet lack the background or the balance to be an effective project manager. Working with others, as you'll learn throughout this book, is the primary key to being effective.

If you have a military background, especially the army, you might have gravitated toward project management because your command unit offered vocational training. Indeed, project management is highly relevant to army work. Military officers know that, in addition to their combat knowledge, being effective as a project manager helps them land a good job after they leave the service.

2. Unschooled Veteran

Perhaps you have been in project management for years and didn't learn the industry jargon. Possibly you had to dive headlong into your first project management assignment. Your "course of study" was 100% on-the-job training, and because you found yourself in a sink-or-swim situation, you learned to swim!

Maybe you now have an incentive to shore up your knowledge and to more fully embrace your role as project manager. Perhaps you have been told by higher-ups to take a course, read a book, or learn more about the profession, so you can develop some kind of structured approach to project management.

If you learned on the fly, you might be resistant to standard ways in which projects are managed. Combining your years of experience with a little "book learning," however, could work wonders. At first you might think, "I'm not going to proceed this way, but it is useful to consider." Still, you'll likely do well with this book, and hereafter.

3. On the Cusp

Are you among those who don't consider themselves to be project management professionals at all, yet you find yourself having to manage a project? Nearly everyone manages a project of some sort—even planning and hosting a party is, in a manner of speaking, "managing a project."

Perhaps you adopted the mindset that says, "There's a whole discipline of thought around managing projects, and I'd like to learn more." You sense that it would be beneficial, both now and for the future, to immerse yourself and gain a better grasp of what project management is all about.

You've been reading books on business management, progressing in your career, perhaps even taking a leadership position, and you find yourself curious about project management. You might be reading *Everyday Project Management* on a plane as you travel for business—you're my kind of reader! You take notes on what you read, discuss the concepts with others, and recommend books to peers when you think it would benefit them. Thanks for all you do!

Pass-Along Power

Considering all the above, whether you're a project manager or soon to be one, you represent this book's primary audience. If you have "pass-along power"—that is, you can assign reading to your staff—my hat's off to you. Project staff members are the secondary audience for *Everyday Project Management* but actually the primary assets to the success of your project. Why? When all project members understand the concepts, terms, basic tools, and importance of cooperation, then group cohesiveness and effective teamwork generally increase, to everyone's benefit.

Committed team members seek to finish projects on time and on budget, with the desired level of quality, and they receive kudos for their accomplishments, much as you probably do. Some project team members will want to read this book to establish a firm foundation. They'll know what other team members know. And they'll want you to see they're taking this proactive step.

Whatever type of reader you might be, it's likely that you're someone who has been in the battle. You've also been exposed to projects that sometimes did not turn out well. You know that feeling, when something is spinning out of bounds. You've seen project team members besieged by requests, and people impacting the group who have different needs and contrasting agendas.

If you've been a project manager and inherited a noncohesive staff, your work can be worse than attempting to herd cats. When a project spirals out of control, it's easy to feel hopeless about it. Still, you don't want to let cynicism overlie your outlook about the potential success of a current project.

Flexibility Is Everything

You're someone who cares about getting things right, and doing things well, both in a world and in an environment where things do not always turn out right. Perhaps your organization unwittingly undermines your efforts, making sudden changes in your staff or budget or project deliverables. Maybe you're asked to do more with less. So, you continually strive to derive new ways to be productive, but, when you've finally got some solutions, someone might pull the rug out from under you again.

One benefit of learning project management fundamentals is that you can employ some of the tools to meet with your boss and, if necessary, deliver hard truths, for example: "If you need me to finish this project a month earlier, it's going to impact quality." To emphasize your point, you could embrace project management tools such as a flowchart or a critical path chart to emphasize to your boss the bottlenecks and impediments to generating the desired results, given the new change in direction or level of resources.

As a project manager, the continuing dilemma that you likely face will be one of changing priorities, budget and resource constraints, the whims of others, or multiple players having an impact. Despite it all, you *can* succeed. Be encouraged that you can handle the vicissitudes of change, and that with the guidance of this book project management won't be so scary. *Everyday Project Management* focuses on what you need to know without overwhelming you, because your job and your life might well be overwhelming already!

1

Project Management in a World of Overload

In this chapter, you learn why having work-life balance is vital to project managers who seek long and prosperous careers, and you discover the importance of learning project management fundamentals. In later chapters, you'll see that when all is said and done, people skills are every bit as vital.

Success, to What End?

What is the value of being successful in your career, rising in your organization, earning ever more salary, and generating praise from many corners, if you don't have a sense of work-life balance? More pointedly, as a project manager, what is the value of bringing projects in on time, at the desired quality level, and on budget; being recognized as highly effective; getting promoted; and looking forward to long-term career success—if you do not achieve work-life balance?

Are you truly successful if each day is a battle? Do you have to drag yourself out of bed, make it through the morning slog, find your way to your desk, and begin again on what seems like an endless series of tasks without a break? Is that a life worth pursuing, deserving of emulation, and the one you sought when you were climbing up through the ranks?

It might seem unusual in a book on project management to first discuss the notion of work-life balance. Yet, to be a successful project manager for the long haul, you need to experience work-life balance on a semirecurring basis. Why only semirecurring? Because nobody lives a life of sustained work-life balance, day in and day out. While you can battle through your current project and maybe the next one as well, despite being out of balance, you actually seek *long-term* career success. So, this otherwise unusual first chapter will prove beneficial.

A Short Quiz

Here is a multiple-choice quiz question: Which word best describes today's typical project manager?

- Overworked
- Underworked
- Energetic
- Lazy

The appropriate answer could well be "None of the above." Powerful social forces have the potential to turn each of us into human whirlwinds, charging about in "fast forward" mode. *Work, time away from work*, and *everything in between* appear as if they are part of an unending, ever-lengthening to-do list, to be handled during days that race by quickly.

The World as We Found It

To say that career professionals in general, and project managers in particular, work too many hours, and that too much work lies at the root of any time pressure they feel and the leisure they might indulge in, is to miss the convergence of larger, more fundamental issues. It's everything else competing for our attention on top of our workload that leaves us feeling overwhelmed. Once we are overwhelmed, the feeling of being overworked quickly follows.

Nearly every aspect of society has become more complex since the year 2000. Traveling is becoming more cumbersome. Learning new ways to increase productivity takes its toll. *Merely* participating as a functioning member of society guarantees that your day, week, month, year, and even life, along with your physical, emotional, and spiritual energy, will easily be depleted without standing at the proper vantage point from which to approach each day and conduct your life.

Do you personally know *anyone* who works for a living who consistently has unscheduled, free stretches? Five factors, or "mega-realities," are simultaneously contributing to the perceptual and actual erosion of our leisure time, including

- Population growth
- The information tidal wave
- Mass media growth and electronic addiction
- The paper trail culture
- An overabundance of choices

1. Population

From the beginning of creation to 1804 CE, world population grew to one billion. It grew to two billion by 1927, three billion by 1959, four billion by 1974, five billion by 1987, six billion by 1999, and seven billion by 2011, according to United Nation sources, with eight billion en route. In less than five years, the equivalent of the current population of the United States, 330,000,000 people, will be added to the planet. The world of your childhood is gone, forever. The present is crowded and becoming more so. Each day, world population (births minus deaths) *increases by roughly 200,000 people,* based on Worldometers calculations. Independent of what type of project you're managing or are about to manage, and regardless of your political, religious, or economic views, the unrelenting growth in human population permeates and dominates every aspect of the planet and its resources, the environment, and nearly all living things. This is a compelling, yet under-acknowledged aspect of our existence, and in a moment I will link them to the four other mega-realities.

More densely packed urban areas have resulted, predictably, in a gridlock of the nation's transportation systems. It is taking you longer merely to drive a few blocks; it's not your imagination, it's not the day of the week or the season, and it's not going to subside soon. Population and road use grow faster than our ability to repair highways, bridges, and arteries.

City planners see no clear solution to gridlock on the horizon, and population studies reveal that metropolitan areas worldwide will become home *to an even greater percentage of their countries' population.* Cities large and small will face unending traffic dilemmas.

The Impact on You—How does ever-increasing population affect your career and your life? Increasingly, it might make sense to live closer to where you work, because commuting in each direction could prove to be burdensome.

It also can be helpful to telecommute more often, so that you don't have to go into the office or visit the project site every day. You can rely more heavily on the tools that we all have in our homes now, including phone, e-mail, texting, logging onto the Internet, and in some cases faxing. Because your project team could be geographically far-flung, you don't meet with them in person on a regular basis, if at all. You could be among those who are geographically distant from the individuals to whom you report. You connect via cyberspace, relying perhaps ever more so on video apps such as WhatsApp or Zoom.

Indeed, sometimes our project team is geographically far-flung because of talent considerations and the desire to keep costs down. If the talent we seek is overseas, and yet can do the job effectively within the budget we've allotted, then by and large that's whom we hire and with whom we work. In many respects, the acceleration of both world population and the "gig economy" are inextricably linked.

You likely already know much of the above, but have you stopped to consider how you could have more-impactful interactions with your geographically dispersed team members or with stakeholders? We'll keep focused on communication issues throughout the text. In particular, Chapter 13, "Reporting Results," focuses on the issues addressed above.

2. The Information Tidal Wave

Many project managers fear that they are under-informed while, paradoxically, being bombarded by information. Over-information wreaks havoc on the receptive capacities of the unwary. The volume of new knowledge broadcast and published in every field is enormous and exceeds anyone's ability to keep pace. All told, more words are published or broadcast in a day than you could comfortably digest in your lifetime.

Increasingly, there is no body of knowledge that everyone can be expected to know. In its 140th year, for example, the Smithsonian Museum in Washington, D.C., added some 942,000 items to its collections. With more information comes more *mis*information. Annually, more than 40,000 scientific journals publish over one million new articles. "The number of scientific articles and journals published worldwide is starting to confuse research, overwhelm the quality-control systems of science, encourage fraud, and distort the dissemination of important findings," the science journalist William J. Broad, of the *New York Times,* once said.

Too many legislators, regulators, and others entrusted to devise the rules that guide the course of society take shelter in the information over-glut by adding to it. We are saddled with 26-page rules and regulations that often could be stated in far fewer pages. Unfortunately, this phenomenon is not confined to government. Nearly-impossible-to-understand software manuals, insurance policies, car rental agreements, sweepstakes instructions, and frequent flyer bonus plans all contribute to the quandary.

Relying on the Best—Information and communication overload most definitely impacts you, and probably does so every day. You have to function in this world like other career professionals. The channel noise, which surrounds each of us, increases inexorably. Thus, it becomes important for each of us, but particularly project managers, to rely on the very best of information sources.

Tune into the best of news shows, and visit the best of web news sites. Rely on the highest level and most credible information sources as often as you can. Have the *mental and emotional strength* to tune out peripheral information that may be interesting or nice to know, but that, in perspective, doesn't support you, your team, the project, your organization, or anything else that's important to you.

Why are both mental and emotional strength necessary? Mentally, recognizing what's best left untouched versus what does merit our attention is challenging enough. Then there is the emotional component. Because we want to be complete in our efforts, sometimes, even when we know an issue is probably not significant enough to devote resources to it, we have a hard time walking away, thinking "It would be so nice to handle that, too." Thus, having only the mental strength, or the emotional strength, often is not enough—you need both.

The strength to let go, particularly in the area of information and communication, will become a skill that you'll want to cultivate and more finely tune as you proceed up the ranks of project management. Why? Project managers, as a breed, tend to be over-achievers if not perfectionists. They want to take care of everything, be on top of it all, and display their prowess, but sometimes that is the path to costly errors, needless diversions, and, on a personal basis, potentially even burnout.

Letting go is often synonymous with abandoning erroneous notions that you harbor. Subconsciously, you could be thinking that if you don't do absolutely "everything" on the project, you'll be harshly judged. People will think you aren't up to the task. Or, you know in your own mind that with a little more effort, you could have included everything! You develop an emotional attachment, unknowingly, to small issues. The risk of this kind of attachment is that you're not going to finish the project on time—this is not likely to be a useful outcome for anyone!

The Center of It All—A project manager is the nexus for the brunt of the information related to a project. So, it's critical to have the ability to prioritize information and assess new information's validity and applicability to the tasks at hand. Project managers are the center of it all: of their bosses, stakeholders, project team members, and perhaps even outside vendors and suppliers—virtually anyone who has a role in the project. Reams of information are directed toward the project manager on a continuing basis, sometimes without a break.

In essence, a project manager has a job-related information overload burden, whether or not it's written in the job description! The temptation to read every e-mail on which you are CC'd can be overwhelming. The inclination to delve into reports, from cover to cover, that come your way, could haunt you as you realize you simply don't have the time to peruse every line of every page. Often, you need to rely on summaries, and sometimes you need to merely skim the information you encounter.

Project managers need to be able to walk away from some tasks without engaging them at all. The ability to prioritize and focus on what's truly important is a vital and emerging skill, for virtually all career professionals, who face a sea of information that is unending. Upper management seeks out such individuals, those who know how to fend for themselves amid so much competing for their attention.

As projects are completed, time passes, and you find yourself assuming more responsibility, the strength to prioritize, weed out, and let go will serve you well. If you begin to develop such skills now, it will be to your great benefit for the many years and even decades ahead.

3. Media Growth

The effect of the mass media on our lives is incalculable. Worldwide media coverage certainly yields benefits. Democracy has a chance to spring forth when oppressed people see or learn about how other people in free societies live. As we spend more hours tuned to electronic media, we are exposed to tens of thousands of messages and images.

To capture overstimulated and distracted viewers, television and other news media increasingly rely on sensationalism. Like too much food at once, too much data, in any form, isn't easily consumed. You can't afford to pay homage to everybody else's 15 minutes of fame. As the late Neil Postman observed, in *Amusing Ourselves to Death: Public Discourse in the Age of Television*, with the three words "and now this . . ." television news can hold your attention while shifting gears 180 degrees.

With a planet approaching eight billion people, media outlets are furnished with an endless supply of turmoil for mass transmission. Such turmoil is packaged daily for the evening news, whose credo has become "If it bleeds, it leads." We are lured with images of crashes, hostages, and natural disasters. Literally, more people die annually from choking on food than in plane crashes or by guns, but crashes and shootings make for great footage and play into people's fears.

The Need for Selectivity—With its sensationalized trivia, the mass media over-glut obscures fundamental issues that *do* merit concern, such as preserving the environment. Meanwhile, broadcasts themselves imply that it is uncivil not to tune into the daily news—"All the news you need to know," and "We won't keep you waiting for the latest. . . ." It is *not* immoral to not "keep up" with the news that is offered. However, to "tune out"—to turn your back on the world in favor of your current project—is not a great solution. Being more selective in where you offer attention, and for how long, makes more sense.

Being more selective is no small feat in an area where you can subscribe to Dish or DirecTV and have up to 400 channels beamed to you via satellite. You can subscribe to various online programming, a variety of Amazon or Netflix services, AT&T U-verse, or other such systems where so many programs and channels can be offered that it's impossible to keep pace.

The obvious solution is to select the handful of channels and programming that best suit your needs and, again, have the strength to let go of the rest. While the amount of programming available exceeds 20,000 hours a week, no one has that kind of time. You only have 168 hours.

Tomorrow, while dressing for work, rather than plugging into the mass media, quietly envision how you would like your day to be and how you would like your project to proceed. Envision meeting and talking with others, making key decisions, having lunch, finishing tasks, achieving milestones, and departing in the late afternoon or early evening. You'll experience a greater sense of control over project issues that you might have considered too challenging. (See Chapter 4, "What Makes a Good Project Manager?")

There is only one party who controls the volume and frequency of information to which you're exposed. That person is you. Each of us needs to vigilantly guard against being deluded with excess data. Otherwise, you run the risk of being overwhelmed by "the latest" issue, and *feeling overwhelmed can exacerbate feeling overworked.*

4. Paper, Paper

"Paper, paper everywhere, but not a thought to think." Similar to too much information, or too many eyewitness reports, having too much paper to deal with is going to make you feel overwhelmed and overworked. Yet, the long-held prediction of paperless offices, for now, is a hoot.

The Thoreau Society reported that Henry David Thoreau, who personally has been unable to make any purchases since 1862, received 90 direct mail solicitations at Walden Pond during a recent year. Under U.S. postal rates, catalog publishers and junk mail producers can miss the target in 98% of the attempts and still make a profit—it has been widely observed that *only 2% of recipients* need to place an order for a direct mailer to score big.

Attempting to contain what seems unmanageable, our institutions create paper accounting systems that provide temporary relief and some semblance of order, while actually becoming more ingrained and immovable, thus creating more muddle.

Maybe One Day—Of the five mega-realities, only paper flow promises to diminish one day as virtual reality, e-books, and online capabilities expand. For the foreseeable future, if you're not careful, you could be swamped with paper, even if you employ sophisticated project management software (see Chapter 11, "Choosing Project Management Software"). It's essential to clear the in-boxes of your mind *and* your desk.

For now, even in this age of voluminous e-communications, paper plagues a preponderance of career professionals. The evidence is plain to see: Look around your own office. How about your desk? Are stacks of paper, often stapled or in file folders, piling up? How about on top of filing cabinets and around the corners of your room?

What about the offices of folks surrounding you?

If paper everywhere and anywhere were not an issue for most people, they would have clear and clean desks, tables, and flat surfaces. Generally, they do not. So, be on alert. Regard each piece of paper as a potential mutineer. Among those sheets with merit and worth saving, electronically scan and file all that you comfortably can. Recycle the rest dispassionately. Each sheet has to earn its keep and remain worthy of your retention.

5. An Overabundance of Choices

In 1969, Alvin Toffler predicted that we would be overwhelmed by too many choices. He said that an overabundance of choices would inhibit action, result in greater anxiety, and trigger the perception of less freedom and less time. Half a century later, we can see and feel that he was right. Having choices is a blessing of a free market economy. For project managers, having too many choices often leads to the feeling of being overwhelmed and can result not only in increased time expenditure but also in a mounting form of exhaustion.

Consider the supermarket glut: Gorman's *New Product News* reports that in 1978 the typical supermarket carried 11,767 items. By 1987, that figure had risen to an astounding 24,531 items—more than double in nine years. Grocery stores in 2018, according to *Market Watch*, carry *40,000 more items* than they did in the 1990s.

Elsewhere in the market, Hallmark offers cards for no fewer than *105* familial relationships. More than 1,260 varieties of shampoo are on the market. Some 2,000 skin care products are available. Even 75 various types of exercise shoes are available, each with scores of variations in style and features. A *New York Times* article reported that buying leisure-time goods has become a stressful, overwhelming experience.

Choosing to Be—Periodically, the sweetest descision you'll have to make might be choosing from what you already have. Choosing to actually have what you've already chosen. Choosing to *be* on your current project. Choosing to work with your project team members. Choosing to tap the potential of your project resources. (See Chapter 7, "Assembling Your Plan.")

Even more important is to avoid engaging in low-level decisions. If a tennis racquet comes with either a black or a brown handle, and it's no concern to you, take the one closest to you. When you catch yourself about to make a low-level decision, consider: Will this make a difference? Develop the habit of making *fewer* decisions each day—the ones that count.

At first, you might feel a bit queasy not making all the decisions related to your project. Happily, this feeling will pass. As you gain more confidence in your project team members, you can rely on them to make lower-level decisions, thereby freeing you to concentrate on the higher-level decisions. In addition, you will likely be a bit gentler with yourself as you begin to realize that letting some of the small issues go will not adversely affect the project, your management capability, or anything else of note.

No Let-up—The rate and volume of change that you encounter on the project, within your organization, and in your personal life are not likely to decline. As we proceed into this brave new world, if anything, you'll encounter more choices with which to contend, not fewer. Thus, you'll need to establish a viable framework for relatively quickly assessing what merits your contemplation and what does not.

The winners in the world of project management understand the importance of focusing on the higher-priority issues. They are aware that spreading themselves too thin can be as risky as not being diligent on those issues that *do* merit their attention. This is, of course, a fine line. Those who become adept at project management learn how to traverse it. Those who don't make it to the finish line, or who do but get close to burnout, are often among those folks who feel they have to stay on top of every little thing. This is insidious. Let go. Trust yourself. You'll be okay!

Overwhelmed and Underserved

In a *Time Magazine* cover story years back, titled "Drowsy America," the director of Stanford University's sleep center concluded that "Most Americans no longer know what it feels like to be fully alert." The phenomenon is now global. Lacking a balance between work and play, between responsibility and respite, we find that simply "getting things done" becomes an end-all: We function like *human doings* instead of human beings.

We begin to link executing the items on our growing "to-do" lists with feelings of self-worth. As the list grows longer, the lingering sense of having more to handle infiltrates our sense of self-acceptance. The world itself seems to be irrevocably headed toward a new epoch of human existence. However, is being frantic any way to exist as a society? To manage a project? To run your life?

We appear poised to accommodate a frenzied, time-pressured existence, as if this is the way it has to be and always has been. Our ticket to living and working at a comfortable pace is not to accommodate a way of being that doesn't support us, but rather to address the true nature of the problem head on. The combined effect of the five mega-realities will continue to accelerate the feeling of pressure.

The positive news is that the key to forging a more peaceful existence can occur for you. *You* are whole and complete right now, and you can achieve balance in your life. You *are not* your position. You are not your tasks. You have the capacity to acknowledge that your life is finite; you can't indiscriminately take in the daily deluge that our culture heaps on each of us and expect to feel anything but overwhelmed.

Balance Begins with the Basics

Viewed from 20 years from now, today will appear as a period of relative calm and stability when life moved at a manageable pace. On a deeply felt personal level, recognize that from now on, you will face an *ever-increasing* array of items competing for your attention, both on the current project and off it.

Each of the five mega-realities will proliferate in the next decade. You can't handle everything, nor is the attempt to do so worthwhile. It's time to make compassionate, though difficult, choices about what is best ignored versus what does merit your attention and action

Work campaigns come and go. Trying times happen. Stretches occur when we have to flat out give our all, maybe to the detriment of other aspects of our life. Such times pass. Concurrently, we need to acknowledge that a life of balance supports people and their careers. Work-life balance includes the basics: good sleep (see below) every night, good nutrition daily, and exercise at least three or four times a week.

Pay heed to these basics so you can be effective on the current project as well as for the long haul as a project manager. Why? Project management is not for the meek. At times it can be taxing. If just anybody could handle it, then many more people would. Thankfully, starting from where you are, you can be effective as a project manager, even if you're on your first project, and still experience work-life balance.

The Quest for Work-Life Balance

What, exactly, is work-life balance? Compared to the legions of instances in which the term is cited, surprisingly little has been written in articles and books about what the concept actually entails.

As the trademark holder and only person recognized by the U.S. Patent and Trademark Office as "The Work-Life Balance Expert®," I regard work-life balance as the ability to experience a sense of control and to stay productive and competitive at work, while maintaining a happy, healthy home life with sufficient leisure. It requires attaining focus and awareness, despite seemingly endless tasks and activities competing for your time and attention.

Work-life balance entails having some breathing space for yourself each day; feeling a sense of accomplishment, while not being consumed by work; and having an enjoyable domestic life without short-changing career obligations. It is rooted in whatever fulfillment means to you within 24-hour days, seven-day weeks, and however many years you have left.

Several disciplines support work-life balance, though individually none are synonymous with it:

- Self-Management
- Time Management
- Stress Management
- Change Management
- Technology Management
- Leisure Management

1. Self-Management

Sufficiently managing one's self can be challenging, particularly in getting the aforementioned proper sleep, exercise, and nutrition. Self-management is the recognition that effectively using the hours allotted to us in our lives is vital, and that life, time, and available resources are finite. It means becoming captain of our own ship: No one is necessarily coming to steer for us.

Self-management is the overarching discipline to all six elements of work-life balance. Unless you're able to successfully manage yourself, how can you manage others, let alone the intricacies of a project? Self-management starts with the basics but then extends to working productively throughout the day, taking periodic breaks, and recognizing which tasks you can best tackle at which times, so you can stay productive nearly all day long.

2. Time Management

Time management is a term that has been in vogue for more than 100 years, although the essence of time management today has changed: Clearly, most people no longer work in factories. Nor do many office workers constantly engage in repetitive tasks. Today, labor and service workers aside, nearly all other workers are knowledge workers in some way or another, as are most or all of your project team members. Tasks change every other day, if not daily. New challenges arise. Often, on-the-spot decisions need to be made.

Effective time management involves making optimal use of your day and summoning all available supporting resources, because you can only keep pace when your resources match your challenges. Time management is enhanced by creating appropriate goals and discerning what is both important *and* urgent versus what is important *or* urgent. It involves understanding what you do best, and when you do it best, and assembling the appropriate tools to accomplish specific tasks.

Many of the project management tasks we tackle are first-time in nature (to us), and so we might not know the actual time needed to complete them. Spending your time effectively means ranking the tasks before you, in order of importance, and then tackling the first one to completion, if possible, before going on to the second task.

3. Stress Management

By their nature, societies tend to become more complex over time. In the face of increasing complexity, stress on the individual is inevitable. Some stress is useful and beneficial, and often that is not the type of stress we even notice. It's what we *do* notice—the kind of stress that impedes us in some way—that requires some attention.

Stress management is a crucial skill in our rush-rush society, where seemingly few moments are available to take a breath. Independent of one's individual circumstances, more people, more noise, and more distractions require many of us to become more adept at maintaining tranquility and at being able to work ourselves out of pressure-filled situations. Many forms of multitasking can increase our stress, while focusing on one thing at a time helps decrease stress.

Without tending to your mental, emotional, and physical needs, stress is predictable. Techniques for counteracting stress include meditation, yoga, vigorous exercise, visualization, and even aromatherapy, among dozens of other methods.

4. Change Management

Managing change is why project managers are hired: In one form or another, each of us is hired or retained to manage change. In today's fast-paced world, change is virtually the only constant. Continually adopting new methods and adapting old methods are vital to achieving a successful career and having a happy home life. Effective change management involves offering periodic and concentrated efforts, so that the volume and rate of change both at work and at home do not overwhelm or defeat you.

Resistance is bound to emerge. People cling to how they've been proceeding even if it's no longer a viable alternative. If you can adapt on the fly, and be effective even as the "rules" change, you will become more valuable to your organization. Forthcoming chapters touch on how to be nimble as unforeseen changes occur.

5. Technology Management

Effectively managing technology requires ensuring that technology serves you rather than confounds you. Technology has long been with us, since the first walking stick, spear, flint, and wheel. Today, the rate of technological change is accelerating exponentially, brought on by vendors who seek to expand the market share for their products or services. Often, as in the case of highly touted project management tools, you have little choice but to keep up with the technological "Joneses." Still, *you* rule technology. Don't let it rule you.

Here are some effective ways to become more technologically adept, without giving up your identity or your life in the process: Each week, learn one new presentation or communication tool, particularly those that are already part of existing software packages that you use. Read at least one article a week related to communication or presentation technology. The article can be in a PC magazine, a business journal, or your local newspaper. Once a month, read a book related to technology. Again, be easy on yourself by picking up books that put technology into perspective in an understandable, friendly way.

Managing technology is vexing to some and old hat to others. I suggest that technology novices team up with technology pros to have an effective reciprocal exchange. Haves help have-nots with technology, and veterans help newbies with insights, observations, and hard-won industry wisdom.

6. Leisure Management

Managing leisure is the last but certainly not least vital discipline. The most overlooked of the work-life balance supporting disciplines, leisure management acknowledges the importance of rest and relaxation—that one can't short-change leisure, and that "time off" is a vital component of the human experience. Curiously, too much of the same leisure activity, however enjoyable, can lead to monotony. Thus, effective leisure management requires varying one's activities.

While we need leisure on a regular basis, many people force-fit leisure between two periods of frenzied activity. True leisure means the ability to wind down, disconnect, and mentally, if not physically, go someplace else that is not connected to work and unrelated to the current project. At least weekly, usually on the weekend, we could use some leisure. Periodically, we need whole vacations that depart from our routines.

Your key to having sufficient leisure all along is learning that you don't need to stay at work longer each day. Indeed, to reclaim your day, you can't stay longer. Your quest is to accomplish what you seek to accomplish within the eight- or nine-hour workday. Then, have life for the rest of the day.

A Brave New World

As we move into the brave new world of ever-accelerating flows of information and communication, the quest for project managers to achieve work-life balance on a regular and continuing basis will be increasingly difficult, yet it's a challenge that's entirely worth pursuing. We owe it to ourselves, to our families, to our project team, and to our organization as a whole to achieve work-life balance.

A world that consists of human "doings"—not human *beings*—scurrying about to get things done, with no sense of breathing space, is not a place where you or I would likely want to live. I don't want to be part of a culture of overwhelmed individuals who can't manage their own spaces or the spaces common to everyone. I prefer not to live in a society, or a world, of time-pressed people who have nothing left to leave for future generations. My guess is that you don't, either.

Eight-hour workdays, 250 days a year, yield a work year of 2,000 hours. Nine-hour works days add up to 2,250 hours. Can you accomplish your projects in 2,000 to 2,250 hours? *Yes!* Thousands of hours, eight to nine hours, even a single hour, is a great deal of time—if you have the focus, the quiet, and the tools.

Achieving work-life balance doesn't require radical changes in what you do. It's about developing fresh perspectives and sensible, actionable solutions that are appropriate for you. It means fully engaging in work and life with what you have, right where you are, smack dab in the ever-changing dynamics of your personal and professional responsibilities.

Make it a choice—Tell yourself, "I choose to live in a society composed of people leading balanced lives, with rewarding careers, happy home lives, and enough space to enjoy themselves."

■ ■ ■

For much of the world, the pace of life will speed up even more. Among project managers, the future will belong to those who steadfastly choose to maintain control of their lives and control of their projects, effectively draw on their resourcefulness and imagination, and help others to do the same.

QUICK RECAP

- As a project manager, the value of finishing projects on time and budget, at the desired quality level; being recognized as highly effective; getting promoted; and looking forward to long-term career success are all enhanced when you achieve work-life balance.

- Participating as a functioning member of society guarantees that your physical, emotional, and spiritual energy will easily be depleted without the proper vantage point from which to approach each day and conduct your life.

- To experience a greater sense of control over challenging issues, each morning quietly envision how you would like your day to be; include everything that's important to you, such as talking with others, making key decisions, having lunch, attending meetings, finishing tasks, and walking away from your office in the evening.

- Only one person controls the volume and frequency of information that you're exposed to—you. Each of us needs to vigilantly guard against being deluded with excess data.

- As you complete projects and take on greater levels of responsibility, the strength to prioritize, weed out, and mentally and emotionally let go will serve you well. If you can start to develop these skills now, you will derive many benefits in the years and even decades ahead.

- Several disciplines support work-life balance, though individually none is synonymous with work-life balance: self-management, time management, stress management, change management, technology management, and leisure management.

2

Industry Norms— Should You Conform?

I n this chapter, you learn why it's worthwhile to gain a rudi-mentary understanding of project management *before* en-rolling in a tech-savvy program or course of study bolstered by software and prevailing project management terminology.

Quiz Question

Besides being regarded as the Seven Wonders of the Ancient World, what do these sites have in common: the Great Pyramid at Giza, Egypt; the Hanging Gardens of Babylon, in what is now Iraq; the Statue of Zeus at Olympia, Greece; the Temple of Artemis at Ephesus, Turkey; the Mausoleum at Halicarnassus, in what is now Bodrum, Turkey; the Colossus of Rhodes in Greece; and the Lighthouse at Alexandria, Egypt? And what do the following sites have in common with the *New* Seven Wonders of the World: the Great Wall of China; Petra, an archaeological city in southern Jordan; the Colosseum in Rome, Italy; Chichen Itza in the Yucatán of Mexico; Machu Picchu in the Cuzco region of Peru; the Taj Mahal in Agra, Uttar Pradesh, India; and the Christ the Redeemer statue overlooking Rio de Janeiro, Brazil? Further, what do these have in common: the Acropolis in Athens, Greece; the Suez Canal; the Panama Canal; the Hagia Sophia in Istanbul, Turkey; Teotihuacan in the Basin of Mexico; the Empire State Building in New York City; the Eiffel Tower in Paris; the Porcelain Tower of Nanjing, China; El Mirador in Guatemala; the Tower of London; and many other notable places around the world?

The answer, in a nutshell, is that they are major architectural, landscaping, engineering, or construction feats that were conceived, built, and perfected *without the aid of a computer, software, or any of the technological tools that are commonly associated with project management.*

The same can be said of the Great Canadian Railway, the Patagonia Highway in South America, the U.S. Interstate Highway System, the Trans-Siberian Highway, the Aswan Dam in Egypt, the Itaipu Dam bordering Brazil and Paraguay, the Hoover Dam in Arizona, the Golden Gate Bridge in San Francisco, the Great Siege Tunnels of Gibraltar, the first passenger ocean liners, all aircraft prior to World War II, early steel mills, and on and on.

To say it another way, long before project management software and spreadsheets—and, regarding the "14 Wonders" named above, long *before anyone knew about electricity*, let alone cyberspace—ambitious civilizations around the globe, spurred on by pioneering builders, devised and constructed some of the most enduring, iconic sites and destinations in the world.

These massive projects involved conception (that is, the genesis of the idea), designing, planning, and material and labor considerations, all of which are part of today's computer-aided world that obviously none of the builders and designers of these projects had at their disposal. As such, not all projects proceeded with the efficiency that today's projects can muster. There were costly delays, high accident and mortality rates, and sometimes gargantuan setbacks. Despite it all, the march of civilization and the proliferation of monumental feats continued unabated.

Modern Origins

The modern-day discipline of project management, to various degrees, sprang from the U.S. military and then spread to industry. To this day, because of the nature of the military, many project management protocols are a bit more bureaucratic in nature than strictly necessary.

This added layer of bureaucracy is burdensome when undertaking a small project. In addition, the certification process of many certifying bodies in the field of project management sometimes overcomplicates issues. Basic knowledge and skills that a person needs to adroitly manage a project are diluted by complex, esoteric, largely unneeded terms and concepts that some project managers might not have to use at all. It's almost as if a person were to buy a new car, loaded with benefits and features, amazing technology and gadgets, and doesn't partake of most of them.

Features Unknown and Rarely Used—Consider the gal who buys the swankiest high-prestige car available. For the duration of her ownership, she drives around town partaking of only a fraction of the car's capabilities. This is all fine, if she's otherwise satisfied, which is usually the case. How much *less* could this woman pay to own a car only with the features and capabilities she'd regularly use?

The project management certifying bodies include complexity in their courses, guidebooks, and resources. Does this enhance the mystique of their brand and overall services? Those who control the terminology that the industry adopts as crucial create an exclusivity for themselves.

Ensnarled by Jargon?

Business literature of the last 100 years essentially repeats many of the same concepts, but continues to coin new terms and fresh phrases to describe such concepts. Why take timeless concepts in project management and put a new spin on them?

What's What among the Gatekeepers—As you read about the terms and items that follow, stay focused on the underlying concepts that they encompass. For example, *Agile* is both a way of thinking and a general approach to management that emphasizes the value of human communication, especially in an environment that constantly changes. It's important to stay flexible on the path to presenting workable, proven results.

Also, recognize that thought-leaders as well as organizations experience various stages of enchantment with terminology and tools. Viewed from a longer-term perspective, even if the *Harvard Business Review* and other top business publications are touting "agile this" and "agile that," over time, the term will fall out of vogue. Everything does, eventually. Here are a few contemporary terms and items you'll likely encounter in the world of project management:

PMI professional certification: "Developed by practitioners for practitioners, our certifications are based on rigorous standards and ongoing research to meet the real-world needs of organizations. With a PMI certification behind your name, you can work in virtually any industry, anywhere in the world, and with any project management methodology. Wherever you are in your career, we have a certification for you."

The *Agile Practice Guide* was created in partnership with Agile Alliance® and offers tools, guidelines, and a compilation of agile approaches to project management. It is designed to steer "traditional" project managers to a more-agile approach. As described in the product literature, the book includes the following sections:

- An Introduction to Agile—describes the Agile Manifesto mindset, values, and principles and describes the concepts of definable and high-uncertainty work as well as the correlation between lean, the Kanban Method, and agile approaches.

- Life Cycle Selection—introduces life cycle varieties discussed in the *Guide*, and explains tailoring guidelines, suitability filters, and combinations of approaches.

- Creating an Agile Environment—focuses on factors to contemplate, such as team composition and servant leadership, when establishing an agile environment.

- Delivering in an Agile Environment—explains how to organize a team and then implement common practices for regularly delivering value. It explains empirical measurements that the team can apply as well as options for reporting project status.

- Organizational Considerations for Project Agility—examines key organizational factors such as culture, business practices, readiness, and the role of a project management office in pursuit of adopting agile practices.

Tinderbox, version 7, is described by the vendor as an expressive, "invaluable tool for capturing and visualizing your ideas." Illustrative, flexible maps enable you to quickly clarify any tangled links you might have. "Natural language processing extracts names, places, and organizations" to help users accomplish more. Improved maps, charts, and flagged terms help users to visualize even intricate "qualitative coding projects."

Scrum essentially is a widely used *Agile* method for managing a project, primarily software development. While Agile software development using scrum might be perceived as a methodology, it actually is a lightweight framework for process management. A "process framework" is a definitive set of practices that must be incorporated for a process to be consistent with the framework.

The Agile Attitude

Understanding Agile takes a bit of, well . . . agility. It is both an approach to management and a way of thinking. What it is not: a list of instructions, a guidebook, or some type of certification. Moreover, viewing Agile as some type of template by which to manage is actually contrary to what Agile is all about.

The Project Management Institute contends that more than 70% of organizations have instituted some type of Agile approach, while more than 25% of manufacturing firms employ Agile exclusively. PMI research suggests that Agile-based projects are nearly 30% more successful than traditional projects.

Agile values doing work in pieces, also known as sprints. These pieces eventually add up to desired results. Agile managers learn from what they have accomplished. The focus of Agile is to produce workable, demonstrable results. To further emphasize, managers who adhere to Agile approaches do their best on the piecework that eventually adds up to a finished product, service, or deliverable. The goal is not to hit a home run on the first swing, but instead to hit single after single to advance runners or, in this case, progress.

Ever Changing

Agile project management is ever-changing. Project managers will define it in different ways, and that could be confusing. A simple way to understand Agile project management is to recognize that it focuses on human communication, being flexible in the face of changing situations, and delivering workable solutions.

A key Agile principle holds that "the most efficient and effective method of conveying information to and within the development team is face-to-face conversation."

Many popular project management software packages are designed with Agile in mind. (See Chapter 11, "Choosing Project Management Software.") "As applied to project management, agile focuses on effectiveness of communications rather than endless meetings, e-mail correspondence, or reams of documentation." With that in mind, if you can successfully communicate with somebody in 10 to 15 seconds of conversation, instead of an e-mail, by all means proceed.

The accent on face-to-face communications over e-communications gives rise to what is known as the daily *scrum,* which is part and parcel of an Agile approach. In essence, a scrum is a communication tool within an Agile framework. As one manager put it, "Scrum is a method for organizing tasks to promote agility."

A scrum can be a 10-minute meeting in which a group stands, not sits, and collectively makes a team plan as well as individual plans for the day. Why is the term *scrum* employed instead of "a 10-minute standup meeting"?

Scrum is borrowed from rugby, where the players huddle quickly and plan for the next play. In football it's called a huddle. In baseball, the infielders meet at the pitcher's mound to discuss the next play. Basketball doesn't have such a term: Teammates will meet anywhere on the court as needed, generally for a few seconds. Scrum, as used in project management, and as applied by Agile and Tinderbox authors, conveys a sense of exclusivity.

Your Bottom Line

Whether it's Agile, team building, customer service, or what-have-you, what are their underlying concepts, and what makes their tenets viable now and for the future? You want to always seek both the short- and the long-term utility of a management methodology, a tool, a system, or even a set of beliefs.

In project management, when you sweep away the contemporary hubbub, an underlying structure prevails. The need to establish order, to marshal adequate resources, to carefully schedule activities and events, all remain vital in any era. That's why this book emphasizes the underlying fundamentals of project management, while acknowledging that today's terminology and tools provide the contemporary template and operating systems by which we do proceed.

When you stay open-minded to the available new terminology and tools, you'll tend to learn new things and gain perspectives that you might not otherwise encounter. So, you'll want to understand the industry jargon, but not be ensnarled by it, as if a particular term were mandatory and so vital that you can't successfully manage a project without it.

Institutional Pitfalls

As a youth, you probably learned multiplication and division first, by hand. Later, you used calculators. If you started with calculators and didn't learn the underlying basic math, you are dependent on calculators and computers for life, and in their absence you're totally stuck, like those who understand little if any math. Similarly, widely touted tools for project management do convey considerable benefits, but first you need to learn the fundamentals of project management, which this book offers.

Agile devotee or not, it's prudent for you to become familiar with the essence of the approach, and to learn the jargon, if only to be able to hobnob with other project managers within your organization and the profession in general.

Standardization Helps and Hurts

The PMI credential is regarded as the industry standard. Significant numbers of instructors in the field teach to this credential, essentially helping their trainees become adept at passing the exam. That's fine, since the PMI credential indicates that titleholders adhere to an industrywide ethical code. Also, standardization of instruction can be helpful in some ways.

Standardization can also potentially be stifling in terms of your applying original thinking, creative approaches, and innovative solutions to project management challenges. On smaller projects, an astute manager using spreadsheet software and simple management tools can do equally well, and perhaps more easily.

Whether you're a beginner or have managed projects for a while, you'll want to be comfortable in various settings. It *is* useful for you to ultimately understand the basic principles of *scrum*, not a topic in this text, but certainly one you will encounter. It's also wise to eventually become familiar with *Tinderbox* capabilities for project planning and other approaches deemed vital by PMI. However, *these are not the first areas* to explore on the path to being an effective project manager.

As discussed in Chapter 1, *balance is vital,* as is your ability to *work with people* and communicate effectively. Once you punch those tickets, then understanding the *basic tools*— including the Gantt chart, flowcharts, and the critical path method (CPM) of project control (topics covered in Chapters 9 and 10)—represents the third leg of the stool to support your efforts.

Underlying Concepts Count

Constructing this book, to reemphasize, required a ground-up approach. In analog fashion, *Everyday Project Management* first examines the tools that people have successfully relied on for at least the last hundred years, including the aforementioned Gantt chart, the critical path method (CPM), flowcharts, and tree diagrams. It then discusses how they can be applied in the work and life of the everyday project manager.

The difficulty of jumping into project management relying totally on popular software, without understanding the underlying concepts, can be illustrated by the following story.

I had met Annie, the VP of Internet Technology (IT) for a major bank with headquarters on the East Coast. She was receiving a salary of $248,000—an outrageous sum in North Carolina a few years back—plus a matching bonus of $248,000, as well as other perks and bonuses. All told, she annually received more than a half million dollars.

It was Annie's standard operating procedure to use her GPS every time she got into her car, even to drive only a few blocks to or from her lavish home. She relied on the GPS to such a great degree that she had precious little knowledge of the streets and larger community in which she resided.

For whatever reason, one day, while she was driving us around town, her GPS gave out. Despite repeated attempts, she could not make it function properly, and she kept no maps in the car. Suddenly, she realized she was lost and this highly intelligent, self-confident, and supremely competent person became unglued. Annie was frustrated with the device, but more so with herself. Not being from the area, I was of little help.

When she got a few blocks closer to her house, Annie began to recognize a landmark here and there, and eventually got home. In perspective: This otherwise ultra-effective, highly rewarded, career professional had relied heavily on technology to navigate about town, without learning the basics—the major roads of Charlotte and the streets near her home. As such, in the face of this temporary glitch, she got utterly lost.

How many other motorists today, I wonder, fail to ever look at a map so as to understand the basics of their own geographic environment, gain some knowledge of their own neighborhood and surrounding community, get familiar with the major roads, and be able to navigate a bit around town without relying on their GPS crutch?

Fundamentals Matter

Even a few blocks from her house, Annie was befuddled until she recognized some businesses and houses. The names of streets meant nothing to her. The fact that she had traversed some of these roads at other times was of little help.

The lesson for budding and as well as seasoned project managers is clear: First learn the fundamentals of project management, which will be covered in this book. *Then* gravitate to the prevailing industry software and enjoy the benefits and features of that software, which *will make your job easier.*

Without understanding the underlying concepts of project management, if you jump into the fray while relying heavily on project and software, be forewarned: You run only a minuscule risk that the software will somehow fail you. What's more likely is that you won't feel fully comfortable in your role as a project manager to the degree that others do, who took the time to learn the basics.

Want Some Fries with Your Order?

If you've been in a fast food restaurant, particularly in an airport, as you're ready to pay for your order, did you know that the cash register keys might not contain numbers? Instead, in many stores, the cash register keys contain pictures of, say, a hamburger, french fries, and a milkshake.

Having cash register keys with pictures can cut down on entry errors. More than that, fast food franchisors often find it difficult to hire competent help. So, they "engineered" around employees' needing to have simple arithmetic skills. As long as a cashier can press cash register keys with the pictures of what customers order, the proper amount to charge the customer will appear.

If the customer is paying by credit card, as happens in airport settings nearly all the time, then the cashier doesn't need to have arithmetic skills at all: The system takes care of everything. One can only surmise what happens on a day when the "cashier" has to rely on arithmetic skills to make change because the cash register malfunctions in some way.

Dependency Is Not Pretty

As a project manager, please don't emulate the person who is overly dependent on tools. You'll want to be the person who can come in and say, "Here's how we'll proceed," whether or not the technology and gadgets are available. After all, during a storm, all the power can go off in your office. Can you still keep going?

At an executive retreat I witnessed, one of the challenges posed to participants was to complete a task without the customary resources at their command, such as cell phones, tablets, and laptops, as well as people resources. The executives who had overrelied on their administrative assistants back in the work-a-day world found themselves stymied when seeking to tackle the challenge on their own, in the raw.

Only a handful of participants were able to plot a path and follow a plan that led to success in completing the task. The rest were up in arms. They had relied for so long on supporting resources that they regarded such support as a given. Now, even in a supportive environment, tackling a rather minor challenge, they were at a loss as to how to proceed. For sure, the ability to delegate effectively is a skill vital to leaders. Still, this tale makes one wonder about the nature of competence and confidence.

Competence and Confidence

The more competent you are, the greater your confidence can be in the work you perform. Likewise, if you are highly confident, that can help to enhance your competence. In all cases, you need to have knowledge of the underlying essentials within a given discipline. Even in the age of ultrasmart calculators and computers, good engineers still know how to use a slide rule.

The proverbial bottom line: You need to have earned your chops, not rely all the time on software. As discussed previously, the language employed to discuss the fundamentals might change. The fundamentals themselves don't change, however, especially in relation to smaller projects, the type to which you'll likely be assigned early in your career will change.

Much is at stake if you're building a bridge, a nuclear submarine, or some other hard asset. The many "givens" to your situation can't be altered, such as the length of the bridge, the number of tons of steel required, or the date the client *must* have the finished product. So, you draw on your basic skills, judgment, and, yes, the available tools of technology. You can't be changing your mind every other day on a project to construct a new, hard asset, because you'll run the risk of, say, stockpiling tons of rusty bolts.

Alternatively, if you're a software engineer or are working on some type of software-related project, you have options. You can traverse different paths, and then abandon them if they don't pay off. You can consider multiple ways of accomplishing the same task. You can add bells and whistles, or exclude them.

You have flexibility because a deliverable, such as software, exists in a virtual world that allows for contingencies.

The *day before* delivery, you can position a banner on the bottom, instead of the top of the page, simply because you want to. Such changes might not disrupt the project. Some users will like the banner at the bottom. Others might have preferred it to be at the top.

You Call the Shots

At your discretion, you can make a change to the software if an overwhelming number of users prefer the banner to be at the top.

For the reasons above, Agile project management software places emphasis on what it terms *user-driven* priority queues and *customer-needs* priority queues.

If you're repairing a bridge, you have to obtain approval by the big bureaucracy—the group dispensing the $10 million or $20 million to complete the project. You're going to incur big trouble if you decide to deviate in a major way, midway through the project.

When developing software, say in Silicon Valley, it's common to scrap one way of doing things for another. At times, a single e-mail from a customer will prompt a firm to turn 180 degrees in what they're developing. As project manager, *you* decide. You can rely on technology tools, but when the dust clears, *you* decide.

Interpersonal and Technological Skills

Equally important to understanding the tools is connecting with the team charged with completing the project. Make no mistake: Interpersonal skills are as critical to the project manager as technological skills.

The project manager reports to others, and has sponsors, constituents, and perhaps well-wishers, all of whom need to be regularly kept informed. The project manager has human resources within the organization—project team members— who could be full-time for the duration of the project, or coming and going. Each project team member needs to have a relationship with the project manager and, likely, with one or more others on the team, as well.

It's been stated in many texts that it's easier to take somebody with people skills and teach them the technical fundamentals of project management than it is to take somebody with technical project management skills and teach them the fundamentals of dealing with people, since they don't already have such capability.

In this book we focus on the underlying technical concepts *and* the people side of project management. Accept this as a truism: *You will not be able to avoid the ever-constant need to work effectively with others. Having interpersonal skills are not optional for the project manager, and indeed will likely be the make-or-break factor in your long-term success.*

QUICK RECAP

- The world is full of architectural, landscaping, engineering, and construction wonders conceived, built, and perfected without the aid of a computer, software, or any of the technological tools commonly associated with project management.

- The basic knowledge and skills that a person needs to adroitly manage a project can be diluted by complex and esoteric terms. So, stay focused on the underlying concepts that key terms encompass.

- Agile is a way of thinking and also a general approach to management that emphasizes the value of human communication, especially in an environment that constantly changes.

- Avoid jumping into project management by relying totally on sophisticated software without understanding the underlying concepts. Otherwise, you might not feel fully comfortable in your role. Seek to be the person who can confidently say, "Here's how we proceed," whether the technology and gadgets are available or not.

- The more competent you are, the greater your confidence can be. Likewise, if you are highly confident, that can help to enhance your competence. It's most useful to have knowledge of the underlying essentials within a given discipline.

- Equally important to understanding the project management tools is connecting with the team charged with completing the project. Interpersonal skills are as important to the project manager as technological skills.

3

So, You're Going to Manage a Project?

In this chapter, you learn what a project is, essential skills for project managers, and what it takes to be a good project manager.

The Elements of a Project

What exactly is a project? You hear the word used at work, as well as at home. People say, "I am going to add a deck in the backyard. It will be a real project." Or, "Our team's project is to determine consumer preferences in our industry through the year 2029." Or, "I have a little project I would like you to tackle. I think that you can be finished by this afternoon."

A "project" is the allocation of resources over a specific time frame and the coordination of interrelated events to accomplish an overall objective while meeting both predictable and unique challenges. It is a temporary endeavor, undertaken to create a unique product, service, or result within constraints of time, resources, and cost. The architect Frank Lloyd Wright once said, "Man built most nobly when limitations were at their greatest." Since each architectural achievement is a complex project, Wright's observation is as applicable for day-to-day projects routinely faced by managers as it is for a complex, multinational undertaking.

Experts cite five major elements that define a project: creation, planning, executing, monitoring, and completion, each tackled in a logical sequence. The creation has to do with defining a scope of work that is to be performed, along with major goals that are to be accomplished. Planning is required to define the scope of work and entails defining each job and each task within each job to be accomplished, the duration of the work, the human resources required, and the materials needed.

Execution equates to working the plan. Monitoring, or command as some call it, entails updating the plan as it is worked. Completion means closing out all open tasks required to reach the desired end. However, when you boil things down, projects can be viewed as undertakings that have multiple elements, including the aforementioned specific time frame, an orchestrated approach to codependent events, a desired outcome, and unique characteristics.

1. Specific Time Frame

Projects are temporary ventures. Projects can last years or even decades, as in the case of public works programs, feeding the world's hungry, or sending spacecrafts to other galaxies.

Projects invariably end, however, because the mission is accomplished or is deemed unreachable or obsolete, or funds dry up, or sponsors and stakeholders move on, or external factors require a shift in focus, or the project is consumed by another project, or any of at least a dozen other reasons.

Many of the projects that you face in the work-a-day world will run somewhere in the range of hours to weeks, or possibly months, but usually not years or decades. As such, the scope of this book will be limited to projects of short duration—say, up to six months, but usually shorter than that.

A project begins when some person or group in authority authorizes its beginning. The initiating party has the authority, the budget, and the resources to enable the project to come to fruition and "make it so."

By definition, every project initiated is engaged for a precise period, although those charged with achieving the project's goals often feel as if the project were going on forever. When project goals are completed, a project ends and something else, invariably, takes its place.

Much of the effort of the people on a project, and certainly most of the resources, including funds, are directed toward ensuring that the project is designed to achieve the desired outcome and be completed as scheduled.

Toward completion or realization of a desired outcome, the project might have interim due dates in which "deliverables" must be finished. Deliverables are something of value generated by a project management team as scheduled, to be offered to an authorizing party, a reviewing committee, a client constituent, or another concerned party, often taking the form of a plan, report, procedure, product, or service.

Deliverables can take the form of a report, provision of service, a prototype, an actual product, a new procedure, or any one of a number of other forms. Each deliverable and each interim goal achieved helps to ensure that the overall project will be finished on time and on budget, at the desired level of quality.

2. An Orchestrated Approach to Codependent Events

Projects involve a series of related events which are divisible, definable units of work related to a project, which might or might not include subtasks. One event leads to another. Multiple events might be contingent on other multiple events overlapping in intricate patterns. Indeed, if projects did not involve multiple events, they would not be projects! They would be single tasks or a series of single tasks that are laid out in some sequential pattern.

Projects are more involved; some could be so complex that the only way to understand the pattern of interrelated events is to depict them on a chart, or to use sophisticated project management software. Such tools enable the project manager to see which tasks need to be executed concurrently versus sequentially, and so on.

A project manager is an individual who has responsibility for overseeing all aspects of the day-to-day activities in pursuit of a project goal, including coordinating staff, allocating resources, managing the budget, and directing overall efforts to achieve a specific, desired result. Coordination of events for some projects is so crucial that if one single event is not executed as scheduled, the entire project could be at risk!

3. A Desired Outcome

At the end of each project is the realization of some specific goal or objective. An "objective" as used here refers to a desired outcome; something worth striving for; the overarching goal of a project; the reason for which the project was initiated. It is not enough to assign a project to someone and say lightly, "See what you can do." Nebulous objectives pretty much lead to a nebulous outcome. A specific objective increases the chances of leading to a specific outcome. While one major, clear, desired project objective is established, in pursuit of it there could be interim project objectives. The objectives of a project management team for a food processing company, for example, might be to improve the quality and taste of the company's macaroni dish. Along the way, the team might conduct taste samples, survey consumers, research competitors, and so on. Completion of each of these events can be regarded as an interim objective toward completion of the overall objective.

Project teams sometimes are charged with achieving a series of increasingly lofty objectives in pursuit of the final, ultimate objective. Often teams can only proceed in a stair step fashion to achieve the desired outcome. If they were to proceed in any other manner, they might not be able to develop the skills or insights along the way that will enable them to progress in a productive manner.

Just as major league baseball teams start out in spring training in Florida or Arizona by doing calisthenics and warm-up exercises, and reviewing the fundamentals of the game, such as base running, fielding, throwing, bunting, and so on, so too are project teams better off honing their skills and capabilities to meet a series of interim objectives and outcomes.

The interim objectives and outcomes go by many names. Regardless of the terminology used, the intent is the same: to achieve a desired objective on time and on budget, with the desired level of quality.

When You Wish Upon a Star—Time and money are inherent constraints in the pursuit of any project. If the scheduled start and stop times—in other words, the time line—is not specific and the project can be completed any old time, then it's not a project! It might be a wish, a desire, an aim, or a long-held notion, but it is *not* a project. By assigning a specific time frame to a project, project team members can mentally and physically acclimate themselves to the rigors inherent in operating under said terms.

Many projects are completed beyond the time frame initially allotted. Still, setting the time frame is vital. If it had not been set, the odds of the project being completed anywhere near the originally earmarked period would be far less.

While the budget for a project is usually imposed on a project manager by someone in authority, or even by the project manager, as with the time frame constraint, a budget serves as a useful and necessary constraint of another nature.

It would be nice to have deep pockets for every project that you handle, but the reality for many organizations and project managers is that budgetary limits have to be set. And thank goodness. You are not Paris Hilton or Kim Kardashian. Budgetary limits help ensure efficiency. When you know that you only have so many dollars to spend, you spend those dollars more judiciously than when you have double or triple that amount.

4. Unique Characteristics

If you have been assigned a multipart project, the likes of which you have not undertaken before, independent of your background and experience, that project is original and unique to you. Yet, even if you have recently completed something of a similar nature the month before, the new assignment still represents an original project, with its own set of challenges. Why? Because as time passes, society changes, technology changes, and even your workplace changes.

Suppose you are asked to manage the orientation project for your company's new class of recruits. There are 10 people and they will be with you for a three-week period, as with the group before them. The company's orientation materials have been developed for a long time, they are excellent, and, by golly, they work!

You have excellent facilities. Your budget, though limited, has proven to be adequate, and you feel up for the task. Still, this project will be unique, because you haven't encountered these 10 people before. Their backgrounds and experiences, the way that they interact with one another and with you, and a host of other factors ensure that challenges will arise during this three-week project, some of which will represent unprecedented challenges.

Project Planning

Projects managed effectively involve the preparation of the project plan, which is considered the basic project document. Indeed, the project progresses and endures based on the efficacy of the project plan.

The project plan is the fundamental document that spells out what is to be achieved, how so, and what resources will be necessary. A well-developed plan offers clarity and direction, and spells what you can identify, up to the present, that needs to be handled to achieve the desired project outcome. The plan aids you in periodically assessing if you're where you need to be, or if you're not, what is needed to succeed.

The basic project components, according to Hallows, are seen in Figure 1.

"With the plan as a road map, telling us how to get from one point to another," says Hallows, "a good project manager recognizes from the outset that a project plan is more than an academic exercise or tool for appeasing upper management. It is the blueprint for the entire scope of the project, a vital document which is referred to frequently, often updated on-the-fly, and something without which the project manager cannot proceed."

The term "scope of the project" or "scope of work" refers to breadth and depth—the level of activity and effort—necessary to complete a project and achieve the desired outcome as measured by staff hours, staff days, resources consumed, and funds spent.

Before laying out the project plan (the subject of Chapter 6), the manager starts with a rough draft "preplan" which

FIGURE 1 Basic Project Components

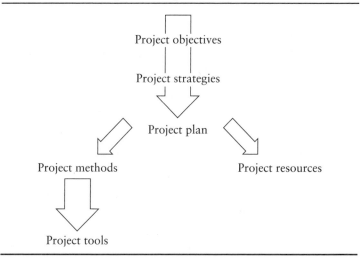

could take the form of an outline, a proposal, a feasibility study, or simply a memorandum. The preplan triggers the project. From there, a more detailed plan is drawn up that includes the delegation of tasks among project team members and the identification of interim objectives, both laid out in sequence for all concerned.

Once action commences and the project team members, as well as the project manager, begin to realize what they are truly facing, the project plan is invariably modified. Hallows notes that "All plans are guesses to some extent. Good plans are good guesses, bad plans are bad guesses." Any plan is better than no plan, since no plan doesn't lead anywhere! No plans are analogous to horrible guesses.

Note that while plans start as educated guesses, they become increasingly accurate and well-defined as the project progresses. Ultimately, you'll gain a good grasp of project goals, which form the backbone of a good project plan.

Project Implementation

Following the preparation of a formal project plan, project implementation ensues. This is where the excitement begins. If drawing up the plan was a somewhat dry process, implementing it is anything but. Here, for the first time, you put your plan into action.

You consult the plan as if it were your trail map, assigning this task to person A, that task to person B, and so on. What was once only on paper or on disc now corresponds to action in the real world. People are actually doing things as a result of your plan.

If your team is charged with developing a new software product, some members might begin by examining the code of previous programs, while others engage in market research, while still others contemplate the nature of computing two years out. If your team is charged with putting up a new building, some begin by surveying the area, others by marking out the ground, some by mixing cement and laying foundation, others by erecting scaffolding, while yet others might be redirecting traffic.

If your project involves successfully training your company's sales division on how to use a new type of handheld device, initial implementation activities might involve scheduling the training sessions, developing the lesson plans, finding corollaries between the old procedures and the new, testing the equipment, and so on.

Regardless of what type of project is at hand, the implementation phase usually is a period of high energy and excitement as team members begin to realize that the change is actually going to happen and that what they are doing can make a difference.

Command

From implementation on, the project manager's primary task becomes that of monitoring progress. Because this is covered extensively in Chapters 7 through 10, suffice it to say here that the effective project manager continually examines what has been accomplished to date; how that jibes with the project plan; what modifications, if any, need to be made to the plan; and what needs to be done next.

She or he also needs to consider what obstacles and roadblocks might be farther along the path, the morale and motivation of her or his staff, and how much of the budget has been expended versus how much remains.

Monitoring progress might unwittingly become the full-time obsession of a project manager intent on bringing the project in on time and on budget. In doing so, some managers lose the personal touch with team members. So, steadfastness in monitoring the project is but one of the many traits necessary to be successful in project management, and that is the subject of our exploration in Chapter 4, "What Makes a Good Project Manager?"

Players and Their Roles

The following are participants you'll likely encounter and the roles that they play in the course of a project:

- Authorizing Party—Initiates the project. (Often called a sponsor: an oftimes unfortunate term, since after initiation many "sponsors" offer notably little sponsorship.)
- Stakeholder—Stakeholders are individuals who are keenly interested in seeing a project succeed and represent those people who'll be affected by the outcome of the project.

  - *Note:* A stakeholder could include the authorizing party, top management, department and division heads, other project managers and project management teams, senior managers, business developers, clients, constituents, and other parties external to an organization. In short, the parties listed above and below, on some level, are all considered *stakeholders.*

- Project Manager—Initiates, then scopes and plans work and resources.
- Work Manager—Responsible for planning activities within projects and servicing requests.
- Administrative Manager—Tends to the staff by ensuring that standard activities such as training, vacations, and other planned activities are included in schedules.
- Team Member—A staff member who performs the work to be managed.

■ Software Guru—Helps install, run, and apply software.

■ Project Director—Supervises one or more project managers.

Effective project management requires the ability to view both the project at hand and all its players from a holistic perspective. By seeing the various interrelated project events and activities as part of an overall system, the project manager and the project team have a better chance of approaching the project in a coordinated fashion, supporting each other at critical junctures, recognizing where bottlenecks and dead ends could occur, and staying focused as a team to ensure effective completion of the project.

QUICK RECAP

■ A project is a unique undertaking to achieve a specific objective and desired outcome by coordinating events and activities within a specific time frame, on budget, and with the desired level of quality.

■ The project plan is the fundamental document directing all activities in pursuit of the desired objective. The plan might change over time. Nevertheless, it represents the project manager's continuing view on what needs to be done, by whom, and when. As the whole team participates in the development and execution of the plan, it becomes more accurate and role players are more invested in the project's success.

■ Regardless of what type of project is at hand, the implementation phase usually is a period of high energy and excitement.

■ Planning leads to implementation; in turn, implementation requires control. An effective project manager constantly monitors progress for the duration of the project. For some, it becomes a near obsession, so the quest to maintain work-life balance is vital.

4

What Makes a Good Project Manager?

In this chapter, you learn the traits of successful project managers, the reasons that project managers succeed, and the reasons that they fail.

A Doer, Not a Bystander

If you are assigned the task of project manager within your organization, consider this: You were probably selected because you exhibited the potential to be an effective project manager. Or, conversely, there was no one else around, so you inherited the task!

In essence, a project manager is an active doer, not a passive bystander. As you learned in the previous chapter, a big portion of the project manager's responsibility is planning: mapping out how a project will be undertaken; anticipating obstacles and roadblocks; making course adjustments; maintaining communications with role players; and continually determining how to allocate human, technological, and monetary resources.

If you have a project team, numbering from one person to 10 or more, then in addition to daily supervision of the work being performed you will probably be involved in some type of training. The training might be once, periodic, or nonstop. As the project progresses, you'll find yourself having to be a motivator, a cheerleader, possibly a disciplinarian, an empathetic listener, and a sounding board. As you guessed, not everyone is qualified to (or wants to!) serve in such capacity.

Beyond these responsibilities, you might be the contact point for support teams within your own organization, as well as with many vendors and possibly suppliers. To free your project management team from an undesired specific task, tasks, or an entire project, you might opt to rely on subcontractors and establish agreements with such vendors for vital services.

Added to these tasks, some project managers also need to engage in a variety of administrative duties. Why? Whether you work for a multibillion-dollar organization or a small business, you might not have all the administrative support you'd prefer to have.

If your staff lets you down or is cut back at any time during the project (and this is almost inevitable), you'll end up doing some of the tasks that you had assigned to others, on top of your planning, implementing, and controlling the project.

Many Hats, All the Time

Chances are that you're going to be wearing many hats, several of which you can't anticipate at the start of a project. A common denominator among successful project manag-

ers is the ability to develop a "whatever it takes" attitude.
Suppose ...

- Several of your project team members are pulled off
  the project to work for someone else in your organization. You will make do.
- You learn that an essential piece of equipment that
  was promised to you is two weeks late. You will
  improvise.
- You discover that key assumptions you made during
  the early implementation phases turned out to be
  wildly off the mark. You will adjust.
- One-third of the way into the project a minicrisis
  develops in your domestic life. You will prevail
  regardless.

Although the role and responsibility of a project manager
might vary somewhat from project to project and from
organization to organization, you could be called on to perform many of these recurring duties and responsibilities:

- Draw up the project plan, possibly present, and "sell"
  the project to those in authority.
- Interact with top management, line managers, project
  team members, supporting staff, and administrative
  staff.
- Procure project resources, allocate them to project
  staff, coordinate their use, ensure that they are being
  maintained in good working order, and surrender
  them on project completion.
- Interact with outside vendors, clients, and other project
  managers and project staff within your organization.
- Initiate project implementation, continually monitor
  progress, review interim objectives or milestones,

make course adjustments, view and review budgets, and continually monitor project resources.

- Supervise project team members, manage the project team, delegate tasks, review execution of tasks, provide feedback, and delegate new tasks.
- Identify opportunities, scope out problems, devise appropriate adjustments, and stay focused on the desired outcome.
- Handle interteam strife, minimize conflicts, resolve differences, instill a team atmosphere, and continually motivate team members to achieve superior performance.
- Make the tough calls, such as having to remove project team members, ask project team members to work longer hours on short notice, reassign roles and responsibilities (to the disappointment of some), discipline team members as might be necessary, and resolve personality-related issues affecting the team.
- Prepare interim presentations for top management, offer a convincing presentation, receive and incorporate input, review results with project staff, and make still more course adjustments.

All the while, you might have to consult with advisors, mentors, and coaches; examine the results of previous projects; draw on previously unidentified or underused resources; and remain as balanced and objective as possible!

Principles to Steer You

In his classic book, *Managing Projects in Organizations*, J. D. Frame identifies five basic principles that, if followed, will "help project professionals immeasurably in their efforts."

1. Be Conscious of What You Are Doing

Don't be an accidental project manager. Seat-of-the-pants efforts might work when you are undertaking a short-term task, particularly something you are doing alone. However, for longer-term tasks that involve working with others and with a budget, acting as an accidental manager will land you in trouble.

Remember that a project, by definition, is something that has a unique aspect to it. Even if you are building your 15th chicken coop in a row, the grading of the land or the composition of the soil might be different from that of the first 14. As Frame observes, many projects are hard enough to manage even when you know what you're doing. They are nearly impossible to manage by happenstance. So, it behooves you to devise an effective project plan that serves as an active, vital guide.

2. Invest Heavily in the Front-End Spade Work

Get it right the first time. How many times have you bought a new technology item, taken it to your office or to your home, and started inputting commands without reading the instructions? If you are honest, the answer is "too often."

Jumping too quickly into project management will put you in big trouble in a hurry. As project manager, you need to understand and recognize the value of slowing down, assembling the relevant facts, and then proceeding—particularly if you are the type of person who likes to leap before you look.

"By definition, projects are unique, goal-oriented systems; consequently they are complex," Frame says. "Because they are complex, they cannot be managed effectively in an offhand and ad-hoc fashion. They have to be carefully selected and carefully planned." He adds, "A good deal of thought must be directed at determining how they should be structured. Care taken *at the outset of a project* to do things right will generally *pay for itself handsomely.*"

Alas, for many project managers, particularly first-time ones, investing in front-end spadework represents a personal dilemma—the more time they spend up front, the less likely they are to feel that they're actually managing the project. As you learned in Chapter 1, too many professionals today, reeling from the effects of our information-overloaded society and feeling frazzled by all that competes for their time and attention, want to dive right into projects much the same way they dive into many of their daily activities and short-term tasks.

What works well for daily activity or short-term tasks can prove disastrous when others are counting on you, a budget is involved, top management is watching like a hawk, and any falls you make along the way will be quite visible.

3. Anticipate the Problems That Will Inevitably Arise

The tighter your budget and time frames, or the more intricate the involvement of the project team, the greater the odds that problems will ensue. While the uniqueness of your project might foreshadow the emergence of unforeseen problems, inevitably many of the problems that you will experience are somewhat predictable. These include, but are not limited to the following:

- Missing interim milestones
- Having resources withdrawn midstream
- Having one or more project team members prove to be not "up to" the tasks assigned
- Having the project objective(s) altered midstream
- Falling behind schedule

- Finding yourself over budget
- Learning about a hidden project agenda halfway into the project
- Losing steam, motivation, or momentum

By acknowledging these inevitable realities and anticipating their emergence, you will be in a better position to deal with them once they occur. Plus, as you become increasingly adept as a project manager, you might even learn to use such situations to your advantage (more on this in Chapter 16, "Learning from Your Experience").

4. Go beneath Surface Illusions

Dig deep to find the facts in situations. J. D. Frame notes, "Project managers are continually getting into trouble because they accept things at face value. If your project involves something that requires direct interaction with your company's clients, and you erroneously believe that you know exactly what the clients want, you might be headed for major problems."

The client might say one thing but actually means another, and later presents to you a rude awakening by complaining, "We didn't ask for this, and we can't use it." Several effective strategies used by project managers to find the real situation in regard to others on whom the project outcome depends are as follows:

- Identify all participants involved in the project, even tangentially involved.
- List the possible goals that each set of participants could have in relation to the completion of the project.
- Identify possible subagendas, hidden goals, and unstated aspirations.

- Determine the strengths and weaknesses of your project plan and your project team in relation to the goals and hidden agendas of other parties to the project.

Following the prescription above, you're less likely either to encounter surprises or to find yourself scrambling to recover from unexpected jolts.

A real-estate developer from Massachusetts says that when he engages in a project with another party, one of the crucial exercises he undertakes is a complete mental walkthrough of everything that the other party:

- Wants to achieve as a result of this project
- Regards as an extreme benefit
- Could have as a hidden agenda
- Can do to let him down

The last item is telling. This developer finds that by sketching out the ways in which the other party might not fulfill their obligations, he is better positioned to proceed, should any of them come true. In essence, he assumes 100% of the responsibility for ensuring that his desired project outcome will be achieved. To be sure, this represents more work, possibly even 50% or more of what many project managers are willing to undertake.

So, a key question is: If you work in project management, and you aim to succeed, are you willing to adopt the "whatever-it-takes" mindset? This doesn't mean that you engage in illegal, immoral, or socially reprehensible behavior. Rather, it refers to a complete willingness to embrace the reality of the situation confronting you, going as deeply below the surface as you can to ferret out the true dynamics of the situation before you, and marshaling the resources necessary to be successful.

5. *Be as Flexible as Possible*

Don't be sucked into unnecessary rigidity and formality. You can view this component of effective project management as a counterbalance to the four discussed thus far. Once a project begins, an effective project manager wants to maintain a firm hand while having the ability to roll with the punches.

You have heard the old axiom about the willow tree being able to withstand hurricane gusts exceeding 100 miles per hour, while the branches of the more rigid spruce and oak trees surrounding it snap in half. The ability to "bend, but not break" has long been a hallmark of the effective manager and project manager in business and industry, government and institution, education, health care, and service industries.

In establishing a highly detailed project plan that creates a situation where practically nothing is left to fortune, one can end up creating a nightmarish, highly constrictive bureaucracy. We have seen this happen at various levels of government. Agencies empowered to serve their citizenry can end up being marginally effective, in servitude to the web of bureaucratic entanglement and red tape that has grown, obscuring the view of those entrusted to serve.

Increasingly, in our high-tech age of instant information and communication, where intangible project elements outnumber the tangible by a hearty margin, the wise project manager knows the value of staying flexible, constantly gathering valuable feedback, and responding accordingly.

Ways to Succeed as a Project Manager

Now that you have a firm understanding of the kinds of issues that befall a project manager, let's take a look at seven ways, in particular, that project managers can *succeed*, followed by seven ways that project managers can *fail*.

1. Learn to use project management tools effectively. As you will see in Chapter 11, "Choosing Project Management Software," and Chapter 12, "A Sampling of Popular Programs," a variety of project management software tools exist today. You'll need at least rudimentary knowledge of available software tools, or possibly an intermediate to advanced understanding of them. The current crop of project management tools can be of such enormous aid that they can mean the difference between a project's succeeding or failing.

2. Be able to give and receive criticism. Giving criticism effectively is not easy. There is a fine line between upsetting a team member's day and offering constructive feedback that will help both the team member and the project. As the saying goes, "It's easy to avoid criticism: say nothing, do nothing, and be nothing." If you are going to move mountains, you will have to accept some slings and arrows. In short, the ability to receive criticism is crucial for project managers.

3. Be receptive to new procedures. You don't know everything, and thank goodness! Team members, other project managers, and those who authorize the project to begin with can provide valuable input, including new directions and innovative procedures. Be open to them, because you might find a way to slash $120,000 and three months off your project cost.

4. Manage your time well. Speaking of time, if you personally are not organized, dawdle on low-level issues, and find yourself falling behind on deadlines, how are you going to manage your project, direct your project team, and achieve the desired outcome on time and on budget?

5. Be effective at conducting meetings. Meetings are a necessary evil during the run of completing projects, with the exception of solo projects. Periodic meetings are vital for keeping project staff informed and for updating superiors on the progress being made on the project. Take the time to read up on the fundamentals of meetings so that you can conduct them in a succinct, enjoyable manner. With a little effort, almost any project manager can become an effective meeting manager.

6. Hone your decision-making skills. As a project manager, you won't have the luxury of sitting on the fence for long in relation to issues crucial to the success of your project. Moreover, your staff looks to you for yes, no, left, and right decisions. Trusting yourself is a vital component in effective project management. If you waffle here and there, you are giving the signal that you are not truly in command.

As with other things in project management, decision-making is a skill that can be learned. However, the chances are high that you already have the decision-making capability that you need. That's why you were chosen to manage this project to begin with, and why you've been able to achieve what you have in your career up to this point.

7. Maintain a sense of humor. Situations are going to go wrong, things will happen out of the blue, and the weird and the wonderful surely will pass your way. You have to maintain a sense of humor so that you don't incur damage to your health, to your team, to your organization, and to the project itself. Sometimes, the best response to forestalling a breakdown is to simply let out a good laugh. Take a

walk, stretch, renew yourself, and then come back and figure out what you are going to tackle next. Colin Powell, in his book *My American Journey*, remarks that in most circumstances, "Things will look better in the morning."

Ways to Fail as a Project Manager

Among hundreds of ways to fail as a project manager, the following seven represent those that I have witnessed far too often:

1. *Fail to address issues immediately.* Two members of your project team can't stand each other, yet cooperation is vital to the success of the project. As project manager, you need to address the issue up front. Either find a way that they can work together professionally, even if not amicably, or modify their roles and assignments. Whatever you do, don't let the issue linger. It will only come back to haunt you further along.

2. *Reschedule too often.* A schedule could be wrong for many reasons, including work incorrectly planned the first time or unforeseen additional work arising once the project starts, both of which frequently occur. So, update a schedule to reflect the real-life situation and to change due dates, assignments, and schedules as needed. Recognize, though, the "cost" each time you make a change: If you ask your troops to keep up with too many changes, you are inviting mistakes, missed deadlines, confusion, and possibly hidden resentment.

3. *Be content with reaching milestones on time, but ignore quality.* Project managers who are laser-focused

on completing the project on time and within budget sometimes don't focus sufficiently on the quality of work done. Let's face it: A series of milestones that you reach with less than desired quality adds up to a project that misses the mark.

4. *Place too much focus on project administration and not enough on project management.* In this high-tech era, with all the sophisticated project management software available, it's easy to fall in love with project administration—ensuring that equipment arrives, money is allocated, and assignments are doled out . . . to the *neglect* of effective project management, which means taking in the big picture of what the team is up against, where they are heading, and what they are trying to accomplish.

5. *Micromanage rather than manage.* This failure is reflected in project managers who play their cards close to the vest and handle most tasks themselves, or at least the ones they deem to be crucial, rather than delegating. The fact that you have staff signals that you personally shouldn't be handling certain tasks and responsibilities. Conversely, if you decide to handle it all, be prepared to work each night until nine, surrender your weekends, and generally be in need of a life. Micromanaging isn't pretty. Able managers know when to share responsibilities with others and how to keep focused on the big picture.

6. *Adopt new tools too readily.* If you're managing a project for the first time while simultaneously counting on a new tool, you're incurring a double risk: Managing a project for the first time is a single risk. Using a project tool for the first time is a single risk. Both levels

of risk are *acceptable.* You can be a first-time project manager using familiar tools, or you can be a veteran project manager using tools for the first time. It is unacceptable, however, to be a first-time project manager using project tools for the first time.

7. *Monitor project progress intermittently.* A ship off course even one degree at the start of a voyage can miss the destination by 1,000 miles. A slight deviation in course early in your project can result in your having to work double time to resume, on track. So, monitoring progress is a project-long responsibility, vital at the outset as cited above, and important in mid and late stages if you want to avoid last-minute surprises.

Any way you cut it, project management is challenging! Plans change. Bosses intrude. Funds don't arrive. Mini-disasters occur. Nevertheless, keep chugging along and keep smiling.

QUICK RECAP

- Project managers are responsible for planning, supervising, administering, motivating, training, coordinating, listening, readjusting, and achieving.

- Five basic principles of effective project management include being conscious of what you are doing, investing heavily in the front-end work, anticipating problems, going beneath the surface, and staying flexible.

- Project managers who succeed effectively give and receive criticism, know how to conduct a meeting, maintain a sense of humor, manage their time well, are open to new procedures, and use project management support tools effectively.

- Project managers who fail allow key issues to fester, neglect to focus on quality, become too involved with administration, ignore management, micromanage rather than delegate, rearrange tasks or schedules too often, and rely on unfamiliar tools.

- Plans change. Bosses intrude. Funds don't materialize. Mini-disasters occur. Keep chugging along. And keep smiling.

5

What Do You Want to Accomplish?

In this chapter, you learn the importance of fully understanding the project, which kinds of projects lend themselves to project management, and why it's vital to start with the end in mind.

The Technical Side and the People Side

Project managers come in many varieties, but in boiling down the two primary characteristics of project managers, they are

- A project manager's ability to lead a team. This is largely dependent on the managerial and personal characteristics of the project manager.
- A project manager's background, skills, experience, and overall ability in handling critical project issues.

If you could only pick one set of attributes for a project manager—either being good at the people side of managing projects or being good at the technical side of managing projects—which might you suppose, over the broad span of the projects ever undertaken, has proven to be more valuable? You guessed it, the people side.

In his authoritative book, *Information Systems Project Management*, author Jolyon Hallows observes, "Hard though it might be to admit, the people side of projects is more important than the technical side. Those who are anointed or appointed as project managers because of their technical capability have to overcome the temptation of focusing on technical issues rather than the people or political issue that invariably becomes paramount to project success."

If you are managing the project alone, you can remain as technically oriented as you like. Even on a solo project, given that you will end up having to report to others, the people side doesn't entirely go away. Your ability to relate to the authorizing party, fellow project managers, and any staff people who might only tangentially be supporting your efforts can spell the difference between success and failure for your project.

Key Questions

In determining what you seek to accomplish, it's crucial to understand your project on several dimensions by asking key questions of yourself, including

- "Do I know the project's justification?" Why do others deem this project to be important? If you work in a large organization, this means determining why the authorizing party initiated the project and, perhaps, whom he or she had to influence prior to your being summoned.

- "Do I comprehend the project's background?" The project does not exist in a vacuum. Probe to ascertain what has previously been accomplished in this area, if anything. If the project encompasses a new method or procedure, what came before it? Is the project of high priority within your organization, or not crucial to operations?
- "Do I fully understand the politics associated with the project?" Politics, in a nutshell, is the relationship of two or more people with one another, including the degree of power and influence that the parties have over one another. So, who will be supportive? Who might not want the project to succeed and possibly be resistant? Who benefits from the project's success? Who might benefit if the project fails?
- "Do I know the players and their roles?" Who will be contributing their effort and expertise to the project? Who will be a bystander? Who will be indifferent?

Nearly every project involves a mix of individuals with differing concerns, values, methods, philosophies, and priorities. A key objective as a project manager, in regards to what you seek to accomplish, is to ensure that the project team maintains coherence and propels the project forward. Otherwise, chaos could ensue.

What Are We Attempting to Do?

A postmortem of failed projects reveals that often these projects were begun "on the run," rather than taking a measured approach to determining exactly what needs to be accomplished. Too many projects start virtually in motion, before a precise definition of what needs to be achieved is even concocted. As the old adage says, "If you don't know where you're going, any road will take you there."

In some organizations, projects are routinely rushed from the beginning. Project managers and teams are given near-impossible deadlines, and the only alternative is for the project players to throw their time and energy at the project, working late into the evening and on weekends. All of this is in the vainglorious attempt to produce results in record time and have "something" to show to top management, a client, the VP of product development, the sales staff, or whomever.

Teams that start in a rush, and accelerate the pace from there, run the risk of being more focused on producing *a* deliverable instead of *the* deliverable. *The solution is to define precisely what needs to be done and then to stick to the course of action that will lead to accomplishing that goal.* In properly defining the project, a few basic self-directed questions help, including the following:

- Have the project deliverables been earmarked? When completed, the deliverables (see Chapter 3, "So You're Going to Manage a Project?"), analogous to outcomes, indicate that the project team is addressing the challenges or handling the issues for which they were assembled.
- Has the scope been established? This involves pinpointing the exact level of effort needed for all parts of the project. Plotting the scope and required effort on a wall chart or with project management software is desirable (the topic of Chapters 9 through 12).
- How will the deliverables be reviewed and approved? Producing a deliverable on time is commendable, but if you do not understand the criteria employed by the

reviewing body, you could run into trouble. The best practice is to ensure that everyone is on the same page from the outset, regarding what is to be accomplished.

Abraham Lincoln, the 16th president of the United States, once said that if he had eight hours to cut down a tree, he would spend six hours sharpening the saw. It pays to spend more time at the outset than some project managers are willing to spend to determine the deliverables' review and approval processes to which the project manager and project team will be subject.

Tasks Versus Outcomes

A recurring problem surrounding the issue of "What needs to be accomplished?" is overfocusing on the project's tasks, as opposed to the project's desired outcome. Project managers who jump into a project too quickly sometimes become enamored by bells and whistles associated with project tasks, rather than critically identifying the specific, desired results that the overall project should achieve. The antidote to this trap is to *start with the end in mind*, an age-old method for ensuring that the project activities are related to the desired outcome.

Some veteran project managers might ask, "How could one have a clear vision of the desired end in sight, or a specific time frame at a specific cost? What if it's not feasible to start with an end in sight?" The short answer: Do your best. By forming a clear vision of the desired end, decisions made by the project staff along the trail will have a higher probability of being in alignment with the desired end. That desired end is not nebulous. It can be accurately described. It is targeted to be achieved within a specific time frame and at a specific cost.

The end is quantifiable. It meets the challenge or solves the problem for which the project management team was originally assembled. It often pays to start from the actual ending date of a project and work back to the present, indicating the tasks and subtasks you need to undertake and when you need to undertake them. Starting from the ending date of a project is a useful procedure, because when you proceed in reverse, you establish realistic interim goals that serve as project target dates.

Telling Questions

In working on projects with professional service firms, one consultant I know asks, "How will you and I know when I have done the job to your satisfaction?" Some clients are disarmed by this question; they have not been asked it before. Inevitably, answers begin to emerge. Clients will say things such as

- Our record-keeping costs will decline by 10% from those of last year.
- We will receive five new client inquiries per week, starting this week.
- For at least two years, we will retain a higher percentage of our new recruits than occurred with our previous recruiting class.
- At least 15% of the proposals we write will result in signed contracts, as opposed to our traditional norm of 11%.

The questions above can be adapted by project managers. For example, "How will my project team and I know that we have completed the project to the satisfaction of those charged with assessing our efforts?" Here's another vital question for project managers who seek success: "Imagine that we've completed this project for you: What are you now able to accomplish?"

The Wide Application of Project Management

In business, many pursuits can be handled by applying project management principles. If you work for a large manufacturing, sales, or engineering concern, especially in this competitive age, worthwhile projects abound; for example:

- To reduce inventory holding costs by 25% by creating more effective, just-in-time inventory delivery systems
- To comply fully with environmental regulations, while holding operating costs to no more than 1% of the company's three-year norm
- To reduce the average "time to market" for new products from 182 to 85 days
- To increase the average longevity of employees from 2.5 years to 2.75 years
- To open an office in Atlanta and have it fully staffed by the 15th of next month

If you are in a personal service firm, one of the many projects that you could entertain might include the following:

- To attain five new appointments per month with qualified prospects
- To initiate a complete proposal process system by June 30
- To design, test, and implement the XYZ research project in this quarter
- To develop preliminary need scenarios in our five basic target industries

- To assemble our initial contact mailing package and test mail within 10 days

If you are an entrepreneur or work in an entrepreneurial firm, the types of projects you might tackle include the following:

- To find three joint-venture partners within the next quarter
- To replace the phone system within one month without any service disruption
- To reduce delivery expense by 18% by creating less complex delivery routes
- To create a database and dossier of our 10 most active clients
- To develop a coordinated 12-month advertising plan

Finally, if you are working alone, or simply seeking to rise in your career, the kinds of projects you could tackle include the following:

- To earn $52,000 in the next 12 months
- To be transferred to the Hong Kong division of the company by next April
- To have a regular column in the company blog or employee newsletter by next quarter
- To be mentioned in *Wired* magazine in this calendar year
- To publish your first book within six months

Notice that all the examples above include metrics. As manager, you become the human representative for the project: Think of it as taking on a life of its own, with you as its spokesperson. At times, you might have to be a nudge, or tighten expectations. Project management involving others is not for the meek!

QUICK RECAP

- Many project managers have an inclination to leap into the project at top speed, without precisely defining what needs to be accomplished and how project deliverables will be assessed by others who are critical to the project's success.

- People represent the critical element in the accomplishment of projects. People-oriented project managers tend to fare better than task-oriented ones. A people-oriented project manager can learn elements of task management. Contrarily, task-oriented managers might find it hard to become people-oriented managers.

- It pays to start with the end in mind, to attain a clear focus of what is to be achieved, and to better guide the decisions and activities undertaken by members of the project team.

- To know if you're on track, ask the telling question, "How will you and I know when I have done the job?"

6

Laying Out Your Plan

In this chapter, you learn the guiding principle of project managers, all about plotting your course, initiating a work breakdown structure, and the difference between action and results (deliverables).

No Surprises

For other than self-initiated projects, it is tempting to believe that the most important aspect of a project is to achieve the desired outcome on time and on budget. As vital as that is, something else is even more important. As you initiate, engage in, and proceed with your project, you want to ensure that you don't surprise the authorizing party or any other individuals who have a stake in the outcome of your project.

Keeping others informed along the way, as necessary, is your *prime responsibility*. When you keep stakeholders "in the information loop," you keep anxiety levels to a minimum. If others receive regular progress reports on your project, and receive bad news early rather than late, then they don't have to be constantly checking up on you. Indeed, many won't be overly concerned. And, if the changes needed do surface, you still have time to incorporate them.

Stakeholders, as previously cited, are those people who maintain a vested interest in having a project succeed, and those who will be impacted by the project or its outcomes. Thus, they could also include the authorizing party, top management, department and division heads, other project managers and project management teams, clients, and constituents, as well as parties external to an organization.

The more you keep others in the loop, the higher your credibility will be as a project manager. By reporting to others on a regular basis, you also keep yourself and the project in check. After all, if you're making progress according to plan, then keeping others informed is a relatively cheerful process. And, having to keep them informed is a safeguard against you allowing the project to meander.

What do the stakeholders want to know? They want to know the project status, whether you are on schedule, costs to date, and the overall project outlook in regards to achieving the desired outcome. They want to know the likelihood that project costs might exceed the budget, the chances that the schedule might go off course, any anticipated problems, and most importantly, any impediments that might loom or that could threaten the project team's ability to achieve the desired outcome.

You don't need to issue reports constantly, such as on the hour, or even daily in some cases. Based on the nature and length of the project, the interests of the various stakeholders, and your desired outcome, reporting daily, every few days, weekly, or even biweekly might be best. (See Chapter 13, "Reporting Results," for more on communications and reporting.)

For a project lasting only a couple of weeks, daily status reports might be appropriate. For projects of three months or more, weekly is probably wise. For a longer-term project running a half year or more, biweekly or semimonthly reports might be appropriate. In any case, the wise project manager safeguards against stakeholders being surprised.

A Plan, Good or Bad

A good plan, to emphasize, indicates everything you can determine, up to the present moment, that needs to be addressed to accomplish the desired project outcome. A good plan provides clarity and direction. It helps you to determine if you are where you need to be, and if not, what it will take to arrive there.

Good or bad, any plan is better than no plan (see Chapter 3, "So, You're Going to Manage a Project?"). With a bad plan, at least you have the potential to upgrade and improve it. But with no plan, you are like a boat adrift at sea, with no compass, no GPS, and clouds covering the whole night sky so you can't even navigate by the stars.

From Nothing to Something

Perhaps you were lucky. The authorizing party might have given you an outline, notes, or a chart of some sort, as a starting point for you to lay out your plan. Maybe some kind of feasibility study, corporate memo, or internal report served as the forerunner to your project plan, delineating needs and opportunities of the organization that now represent clues as to what you need to perform on your project.

Often, though, no such preliminary documents are available. You receive your marching orders from an eight-minute conference with your boss, or via e-mail, or over the phone. When you query your boss for some documentation, he or she offers a couple of pages from a file folder. Whatever the origin of your project, you have to start somewhere.

Many project managers find value in starting with the end in mind, even if many of the details of getting there are only sketchy. As such, they consider these kinds of questions:

- What is the desired final outcome?
- When does it need to be achieved?
- What is the total budget?

From there, consider what is the scope, how wide need you cast the net, and how deep is your sea? By starting with major known elements of the project, you begin to fill in your plan, in reverse (see Chapter 5, "What Do You Want to Accomplish?"), leading back to this actual day. We'll cover the use of software in Chapter 11, "Choosing Project Management Software," and Chapter 12, "A Sampling of Popular Programs." For now, we'll proceed as if pen and paper, or a simple spreadsheet, is all you have. Later, you can transfer the process to your most suitable format.

A Journey of 1,000 Miles

In establishing your plan, as project manager your key challenge is to ascertain the relationship of different tasks or events to one another, and then to coordinate them so that the project is executed in a cost-effective and efficient manner. In laying out your plan, you could end up with 10 steps, 50, or 150 or more.

Some people call each step a *task*, while some prefer to use the term *event*, because not each step represents a pure task. Sometimes a step merely represents something that has to happen. Subordinate activities to the events or tasks are subtasks. There can be numerous subtasks to each task or event.

The primary planning tools in plotting your path, as briefly introduced in Chapter 2, "Industry Norms—Should You Conform?," are the work breakdown structure (WBS), the Gantt chart, and the critical path method (CPM), all of which represent a schedule network. A *path* is a chronological sequence of tasks, each dependent on predecessors. The critical path is the longest complete path of a project. This balance of this chapter focuses on the work breakdown structure. I'll address the other tools in Chapter 9, "Gantt Charts," and Chapter 10, "Critical Path Method."

A *work breakdown structure* consists of a complete depiction of the tasks necessary to achieve successful project completion. Project plans, which highlight the tasks that need to be accomplished to successfully complete a project, are vital, from which scheduling, delegating, and budgeting are derived.

You and Me against the World?

Maybe you're alone and staring at a blank page, or perhaps your boss is helping you. Possibly an assistant project manager or someone who will be on the project management team is helping you lay out your plan. If someone is working with you, or if you have someone who can give you regular feedback, that is to your extreme benefit. Not receiving regular feedback is risky!

Depending on the duration and complexity of your project, it is difficult to lay out a comprehensive plan that takes into account all aspects of the project, every critical event, associated subtasks, and the coordination of everything. To emphasize: If you can acquire any help in plotting your path, take it!

In laying out your plan, consider the big picture of what you want to accomplish, and then, to the best of your ability, divide up the project into phases. By chunking out the project into phases, you have a better chance of not missing anything. How many phases? That depends on the project, but usually it is between two and five.

With help or without it, here is a succinct way to proceed with your plan: List all jobs that need to be accomplished to attain the desired outcome. For each job, list a series of tasks in logical sequences to accomplish it. For each task, estimate a duration, resources required to perform it, and cost of materials. Use the total duration of the job, times the human resources required to determine the cost. *Note:* All such information can be consolidated by using a planning program.

The Work Breakdown Structure (WBS)

The WBS has become synonymous with a task list. Observe that the term "work breakdown" structure has the accidental double meaning of "breaking down" (as in no longer working, and bringing progress to a halt). However, use of this traditional term prevails and, as employed here, it refers to a positive, preferred tool for effectively managing projects.

The basic activities involved in completing the WBS are as follows:

- Identify the events or task and subtasks associated with them. They are paramount to achieving the desired objective.
- Plot them, using an outline, tree diagram, or combination thereof to determine dependencies or an efficient sequence.
- Estimate the level of effort required, usually in terms of person-days, and start and stop times for each task and subtask.

- Identify supporting resources and when they can be available, how long they are at your service, and when and how they must be returned.
- Establish a budget for the entire project, for phases if applicable, and perhaps for specific events or tasks.
- Assign target dates for the completion of events or tasks.
- Establish a roster of deliverables, many of which are presented in accordance with achieving milestones.
- Obtain approval of your plan from the authorizing party—the last item in Figure 2.

In Many Forms

The simplest form of WBS is the outline, although it can also appear as a tree diagram or other chart. Think of the WBS as your initial planning tool for meeting the project objective(s) on the way to that final, singular, sweet triumph.

Sticking with the outline, the WBS lists each task, each associated subtask, each milestone, and each deliverable. The WBS can be used to plot assignments and schedules as well as to maintain focus on the budget. Figure 2 shows a simple example of such an outline.

A *Project Environment* chart, such as that in Figure 3, is particularly useful when your project has a lot of layers, such as when many subtasks contribute to the overall accomplishment of a task, which in turn contributes to the completion of a phase, which leads to another phase, which ultimately leads to project completion.

A *Tree Diagram*, such as the one shown in Figure 4, represents a high-level summary of the key elements of a work breakdown structure (WBS). A full WBS, by contrast, presents tasks, duration, description of tasks, beginning and ending dates, staff responsibilities, and the budgeted amount.

FIGURE 2 WBS Outline

"To Write a Story about a Murder Case"
Source: Copyright Jolyon Hallows

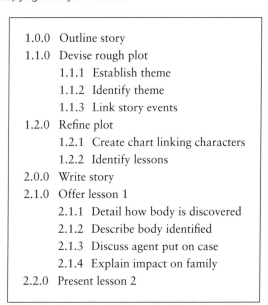

1.0.0 Outline story
1.1.0 Devise rough plot
      1.1.1 Establish theme
      1.1.2 Identify theme
      1.1.3 Link story events
1.2.0 Refine plot
      1.2.1 Create chart linking characters
      1.2.2 Identify lessons
2.0.0 Write story
2.1.0 Offer lesson 1
      2.1.1 Detail how body is discovered
      2.1.2 Describe body identified
      2.1.3 Discuss agent put on case
      2.1.4 Explain impact on family
2.2.0 Present lesson 2

FIGURE 3 The Project Environment

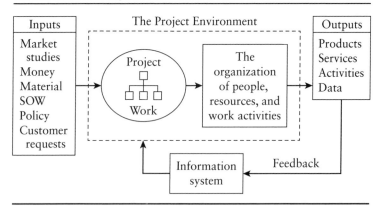

Inputs	The Project Environment	Outputs
Market studies Money Material SOW Policy Customer requests	Project / Work → The organization of people, resources, and work activities	Products Services Activities Data

Information system — Feedback

FIGURE 4 Tree Diagram

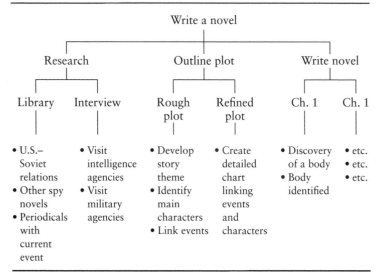

Maintaining a Project Outline

The WBS allows you the opportunity to break tasks into individual components. This gives you a firm grasp of what needs to be done even at the lowest of levels. Hence, the WBS aids in scheduling, doling out, and even budgeting for assignments.

Details, Details

How many levels of tasks and subtasks should you have? It depends on the project's complexity. While scads of details could seem overwhelming, if your work breakdown structure is well organized, you will have positioned yourself to handle even challenging projects, such as hosting next year's international convention, finding a new type of fuel injection system, or coordinating a statewide volunteer effort.

By heaping on the level of detail, you increase the chances that you'll handle all or most aspects of the project. The potential risk of having too many subtasks is that you might become bogged down in details and overly focused on tasks, not outcomes! Fortunately, as you proceed in execution, you find that some of the subtasks (and sub-subtasks) are taken care of as a result of some other action.

Some project managers contend that there is no such thing as "too many" subtasks. You plan the work that you know has to be done. The people who do the work rely on these lists of tasks and subtasks. While the level of detail is up to you, as a general rule the smallest of subtasks to be listed in the WBS would be synonymous with the smallest unit that you as the project manager need to manage. For example, ensuring that some needed supplies were on hand at the appropriate time could well make your list.

Generally, it is better to have listed more details than fewer. If you haven't plotted all that you can foresee, then once the project commences, you might be beset by burdensome challenges because you understated the work that needs to be performed. Or, you might experience unnecessary delays because someone didn't recognize the importance of having some crucial item on hand.

Team-Generated Subtasks?
Could your project management team devise their own sub-work breakdown structures to pinpoint their individual responsibilities and, thus, have a greater level of detail than your WBS? Actually, yes. Ideally, you empower your staff to effectively execute delegated responsibilities. Within those assignments, considerable leeway often exists as to how the assignments are performed best. The net result, often, is that a WBS established in collaboration is a far more accurate tool.

Your forward-thinking project team members might naturally gravitate toward their own mini-WBS. Often, good team members devise subtask routines that exceed what you actually need to preside over as project manager—unless the procedure happens to be worth repeating with other project team members or on other projects in the future.

The Functional WBS

In the example shown in Figure 5, the WBS is divided into separate functions. This method of plotting the WBS is particularly effective for project managers presiding over team members who could also be divided based on functional lines. In this case, the WBS gives a quick and accurate snapshot of how the project is divided up and which teams are responsible for what.

FIGURE 5 Combination Tree Diagram and Outline WBS

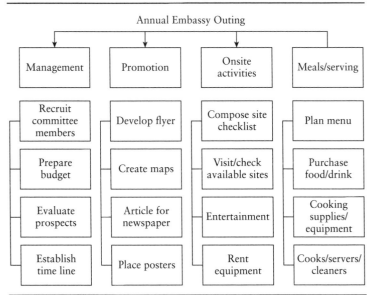

FIGURE 6 Segment of an Outline and Tree Outline WBS

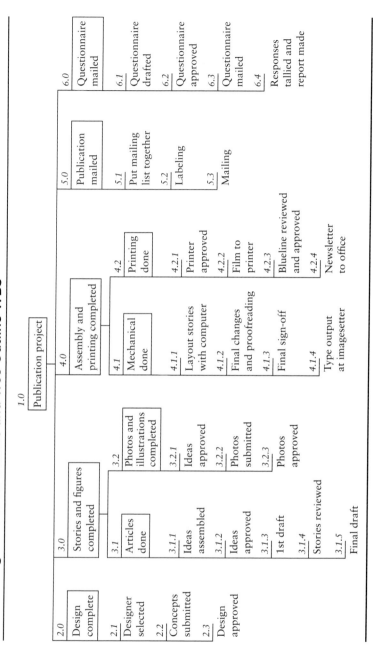

As you can observe, each form of WBS, outline, and tree diagram offers different benefits and has different shortcomings. For example, the outline is more effective at conveying minute levels of detail toward the achievement of specific tasks. When many subteams exist within an overall project team, and each one has specific responsibilities, an outline can be unwieldy, because it doesn't visually separate activities according to functional lines.

The tree diagram WBS shown in Figure 6 visually separates functional activities. Its major shortcoming is that to convey high levels of task detail, the tree diagram would be huge. All the tasks and subtasks of all the players, in all the functional departments, would necessitate constructing a large and complex chart.

Such a chart is actually a hybrid of the detailed outline and the tree diagram. Nevertheless, for various reasons many project managers resort to this technique. By constructing both an outline and a tree outline WBS, and then combining the two, however large and unwieldy the combination becomes, you end up with a single document that illustrates the totality of the entire project.

More Complexity, More Help

With this potential level of detail for your project, it is vital to obtain help when first laying out your plan. Even relatively small projects of short duration could require accomplishing a variety of tasks and subtasks.

Eventually, each subtask requires an estimate of labor hours: How long will it take for somebody to complete it, and what will it cost? (See Chapter 7, "Assembling Your Plan.") You will have to determine how many staff hours, staff days, staff weeks, and so on, will be needed, based on the plan that you've laid out. From there, you could run into issues concerning which individuals you'll be able to recruit, how many hours your staff members will be available, and the project costs per hour or per day.

Preparing your WBS also provides you with a preview of which project resources might be required beyond human resources. These could include computer equipment, other tools, office or plant space and facilities, and so on.

If your plotted tasks and subtasks reveal that project staff will be traveling in pursuit of the desired outcome, then auto and airfare costs, room and board, and other associated travel expenses need to be considered. If certain portions of the project will be farmed out to subcontractors or non-project staff, associated costs will accrue as well.

What Should We Deliver?

Completing project milestones, often associated with the completion of a project deliverable, is an indicator that you are on target for completing the project successfully. Deliverables can take a wide variety of forms. Many deliverables are actually related to project reporting. These could include, but are not limited to

- *A list of deliverables.* One of your deliverables could be a compendium of all other deliverables!
- *The desired end product or service* as a result of the project.
- *A quality assurance plan.* If your team is empowered to design something that requires exact specifications— perhaps some new engineering procedure, product, or service offering—how will you ensure requisite levels of quality?
- *A schedule.* Schedules can be deliverables, particularly when your project has multiple phases and you

are only in the first phase or the preliminary part of the first phase. It then becomes understood that as you delve into the project, you will gain a fuller understanding of what can be delivered and when. Hence the schedule itself can become a much-anticipated deliverable.

- *The overall budget, estimates, your work plan, cost benefit analysis, and other documentation* can all be deliverables, also. A cost benefit analysis is a determination of whether to proceed based on the monetary amounts, time, and resources required for the proposed solution versus the desirability of the outcome or outcomes.

Another type of deliverable centers on acquisition and procurement. A government agency or a large contractor could empower a project manager and the project management team to develop requests for proposals (RFPs), invitations to bid, or requests for estimates as project deliverables. Once the proposals or bids come in, proposal evaluation procedures have to be in place. The following are examples:

- Software evaluation plans
- Maintenance plans
- Hardware and equipment evaluation plans
- Assessment tools

The wide variety of other deliverables might include

- Business guidelines
- Lexicon or dictionary
- Buy-versus-make analysis
- A phase-out plan
- Training procedures

- Product prototype
- Implementation plans
- Reporting forms
- Application
- Product specifications
- Close-out procedures

- Documentation
- Software code
- Experimental design

- Test results
- Process models

It's Results That Count

In preparing the WBS and associated deliverables, you need to focus on results and *not* on activities. The plan that you initiate and further develop becomes the operating manual for the project team.

One project manager on a new software project requested that team-member programmers develop a certain number of lines of code per day in one phase of a project. She felt that this would be a useful indicator of the level of productivity of her individual project team members.

In their efforts to be productive members of the project team, the programmers developed many new lines of code each day. The result, however, was riddled with errors and insufficient for completing that phase of the project. It put the overall project way behind schedule and behind budget.

Rather than making task and subtask assignments related to the number of lines of new code developed, the tasks and subtasks should have reflected code that accomplished a specific, observable capability that led to the project goal. Then, project programmers would have concentrated on code efficiency and viability, as opposed to volume. Often, it's quality, not quantity, that counts.

Supporting Tools

When laying out your plan, you're bound to experience many starts and stops, redirections, and second thoughts. If you have a white board, on which you can simply write down your current thoughts and have them stored to disc and printed later, then you already know that form of documentation is valuable.

Many people simply use stick-em pads, often as large as three by five inches. An event or task can be confined to one stick-em note, with associated subtasks on that same note or an attached note. These can then be moved around at will, either on paper or on a white board, as you are plotting out your plan.

Stick-em pads certainly can be used in combination with a white board. Simply stick them in place (or the best place you can determine at the moment). If you don't have a white board, you can also use a copying machine or scanner to take a snapshot of your current thinking.

To further ease your burden, you can use colors. These could include different colored stick-em notes, colored dots, magic markers, flares, and highlighters. Each event or task could be a different color, or like subtasks could be a uniform color. The options are unlimited and are basically your choice.

Many project managers find it useful and convenient to use colors to track the responsibilities of individual project team members. For example, everything that Scott is responsible for will be in orange and everything Monica works on will be green.

Some project managers find it convenient to number tasks and subtasks. Keep it simple, however, when numbering tasks or subtasks. You don't want to end up with outline structures such as 1-1.2.34, where your task sequence might be more confusing than not having them numbered at all.

Bounce Your Plan off Others

After you've laid out what you feel is a comprehensive plan that will accomplish the mission, bounce it off others—even those who for one reason or another were not available to participate in it. You don't want to fall so in love with your WBS that you can't accept the input of others, or worse, don't even see the flaws. Remember, the more involved your project is, the easier it is to miss something!

- You want people to give it a critical eye.
- You want to have them play devil's advocate.
- You want them to challenge you.
- You want them to question you as to why you went left instead of right.

Maybe they quickly see something that you flat-out missed. Perhaps they can suggest a way to combine several subtasks into one. Possibly they can point out where you've been using ill-matched metrics or the wrong skill level. Or they can identify where you lack buy-in checkpoints with stakeholders.

■ ■ ■

In the next chapter, we add flesh and bones to your WBS, and focus on assigning staff, establishing time frames, and setting a budget.

QUICK RECAP

- Regardless of how worthy your project and how brilliant your plan are, keeping others informed along the way, as necessary, is your prime directive.
- Carefully scoping out the project and laying out an effective project plan minimizes the potential for surprises, reveals what needs to be done, provides clarity, and offers direction.
- The WBS (work breakdown structure) is a primary planning tool in plotting your path.
- The WBS lists each task, each associated subtask, milestones, and deliverables, and also can be used to

plot assignments and schedules and to maintain focus on the budget.

- You don't want to fall so in love with your WBS that you can't accept the input of others, possibly leading you to miss major flaws.

7

Assembling Your Plan

In this chapter, you learn how to further refine your work breakdown structure (WBS), decide whether your labor should be part of the WBS, find out the importance of reintegrating project staff as the project winds down, and discover distinctions between the WBS and other planning tools.

The Critical Path for Completing the WBS

Before a project was assigned to you, an authorizing party or committee determined that it needed to be executed. They allocated resources to the project. At the least, this included costs of your services. They might have also formally or informally made assignments of plant, equipment, and human resources to the project.

At some point you were summoned. You discussed the desired objective, how long the project will take, the key events in pursuit of the final objective, and if the project is best approached via distinct phases. Perhaps a feasibility study was already done. Maybe there were notes and other documents that enabled you to achieve a running start as to what you would be required to do. Often, your initial assignment is to define your own role and present your definition to the authorizing party or committee.

Once the decision was made to launch the project, and as soon as you were given the formal go-ahead, the order of the day became laying out your plan, developing the WBS, and presenting to your superiors, as depicted in Figures 7 and 8.

The Chicken or the Egg?

Preparation of your WBS and the actual commencement of project activities is a chicken-versus-egg issue. For example, many experts advise that you first identify staffing resources and then proceed with the work breakdown structure. Following that approach, the opportunity to allocate staff as necessary comes first, followed closely by budget allocations.

Until you plot exactly what needs to be done, however, you can't allocate staff hours. Some experts advise creating the WBS independently of staff allocations. Essentially,

FIGURE 7 Laying out the Plan, 1

Item	J	F	M	A	M	J	J	A	S	O	N	D
Project launch	▭											
Sponsor approval	□											
Plan development		□										
WBS			□									
Presentation and approval			▯									
Implementation					▭▭▭▭							

FIGURE 8 Laying out the Plan, 2

Item	J	F	M	A	M	J	J	A	S	O	N	D
WBS			☐									
Task			☐									
Precedences			☐									
Assignment			☐									
Resources			☐									
Budget			☐									
Approval			☐									

you identify what needs to be done, and then you assemble the requisite staff resources based on the plan that you've devised. I recommend the latter, because it is a prudent approach to laying out and assembling your plan—you identify needs first and then allocate appropriate staff resources.

When does it make sense to start with the staff in mind?

- When they are all full-time
- When the project is relatively short
- When the project is labor intensive or requires a lot of expensive equipment
- When you likely have the needed skills and experiences within the existing allocated staff

Is Planning Itself a Task?

Another chicken-versus-egg issue to consider is if planning itself represents a task to be included on the WBS. Experts argue that especially for large and involved projects, planning can represent a variety of tasks or events, or even subtasks. Planning can even be synonymous with a project phase. For example, depending on what you're trying to achieve, the outcome of Phase I might be to develop a plan that will be crucial to the execution of Phase II. One project manager for a large company contends that planning is definitely a task and that it needs to be incorporated into the WBS. "Does it not take human resources as well as time to plan?" he asks.

Some critics argue that while planning does consume time and budgetary resources, it is not appropriate to incorporate it into the WBS. They say that the WBS and any other type of planning document merely represent the outcomes of the planning process. A plan is considered completed only when the project actually begins. Thus, the work of the project itself is separate from the plan that enabled the work to commence.

On this particular chicken-versus-egg issue, you decide whether you want to include the planning of the project as a task or event in itself, or simply have it represent a prelude activity for the actual work of the project. As an option, Phase 0 could be planning and buy-in, and what's next is Phase 1. In any case, you can't skirt chicken-versus-egg issues, as they could make a significant impact on your budget and overall plans if you don't consider them.

What about Your Own Hours?

Should your activities and contributions to the project as project manager be listed in the work breakdown structure? Some experts say no. They argue that project management represents pure management—it's there from the beginning; it will be there at the end, and

- It is ongoing.
- It isn't a task.
- There are no milestones or deliverables attached to it.
- There are no events or activities dependent on project management per se.

Those who argue the opposite—that project management needs to be plotted in the WBS—note that though the four bulleted items above might be in effect, the act of managing a project is a vital project input, and it

- Involves labor.
- Consumes resources.
- Helps to achieve outcomes.
- Is clearly a valuable resource.
- Is part of the overall budget (in the form of the project manager's salary).

For these reasons, I advocate that the project management function of a project be included in the work breakdown structure.

Internal Resources Versus External Resources

As arduous as it could seem, constructing a WBS is relatively easy when all or most of the resources are internal, such as your staff, equipment, and other components supporting project efforts.

What about when you have to rely on external resources—outside vendors, consultants, part-time or supplemental staff, rented or leased facilities, and rented or leased equipment? Then the job becomes more involved: External project resources are more difficult to budget, schedule, and incorporate at precisely the right time.

It can also be argued that monitoring the work of outside vendors, consultants, or supplemental staff is more challenging than working with internal staff. Concurrently, external human resources who bill on an hourly or daily basis have a strong incentive to perform admirably, on time, every time.

Helping Your Staff When It's Over

In perfecting your WBS, have you accounted for the reintegration of your project staff back into other parts of the organization as the project comes to a close? This is an issue that even veteran project managers overlook. On some projects, the staff work a uniform number of hours for much of the project. If the project veers off plan, perhaps they work longer until the project is back on course. Sometimes, project staff work steadfastly right up to the final project outcome.

The WBS needs to reflect the added measure of staff meetings, reviews, and one-on-one encounters that are often vital to maintaining performance near the end of a project. By design, since your project is a temporary engagement with a scheduled end, it is logical also to assume that the fate and the future activity of project team members need to be determined before the project ends.

The project manager who overlooks the concerns of project staff, who naturally wonder about their immediate futures, will find that as the project draws to a close, they could start to lose focus or perhaps display symptoms of divided loyalty. Project staff are justifiably concerned about what they will be doing next, whether it's moving on to a new project or gravitating back to their previous positions. You can't blame them, because they have their own career and own futures to be concerned about.

Abrupt changes in job status, such as working full bore on a project to a nebulous status, can be quite disconcerting to employees. Equally challenging for the project manager is when the brunt of the project work occurs sometimes before the actual completion date. Thus, many project staff members might be in a wind-down phase, having worked 40+ hours a week on the project at its midpoint and now, perhaps, spending 20 or less a week on it. They then devote the rest of their time to some other project, or they return to their old position.

In such cases, the project manager needs to account for issues related to diverted attention, divided loyalties, and perhaps leading several project staffers who simply don't have their "heads" in the project anymore. Remedies are available, however, such as meeting with each team member, one-on-one, to solicit their ideas and perspectives, or holding a half-day, team member input session offsite.

What Kinds of Tasks Constitute the WBS?

Whether you employ an outline, tree, or combination WBS, it's useful to acknowledge distinctions between types of tasks. *Parallel tasks* can be undertaken at the same time as other tasks, without impeding the project. For example, you might have several teams working on different elements of the project that are not time or sequence related. Hence, they can all be making progress without impeding any of the other teams. While parallel tasks represent two or more tasks that can be undertaken at the same time, this doesn't imply that they have the same starting and ending times.

Dependent tasks are those that can't begin until something else occurs. If you are constructing a building, you first have to lay the foundation. Then, you can build the first floor, the second, and then the third. Obviously, you can't start with the fifth floor and then move to the third, at least not in three-dimensional space as we know it. So, a dependent task is a task or subtask that can't be initiated until a predecessor task or several predecessor tasks are finished, while a predecessor task is one that has to be completed before another task can commence.

The WBS is not a useful tool for identifying the relationship between *interdependent tasks*. When preparing a WBS outline, you want to proceed in chronological order, much like your progression along a tree diagram. When you combine the outline and tree diagram type WBS, you end up with an extended outline describing the tasks and subtasks associated with the elements on the tree diagram. A full WBS, by contrast, includes the sequence and interdependence among tasks. As such, it can be employed to create a network diagram.

You can then alter the position of the boxes (see Figures 7 and 8) to be in alignment with what takes place and when. Hence, parallel tasks are on the same position on the chart. As you can see in Figure 9, some items, such as assignments and resources, occur simultaneously.

FIGURE 9 Laying out the Plan, 3 (adding detail to the WBS sequence)

Item	J	F	M	A	M	J	J	A	S	O	N	D
Task A												
Task B												
Task C												
Task D												

Dependent tasks necessarily have to have staggered positions. These can be joined by the arrows that indicate the desired path of events or activities. *Milestones* don't necessarily require any time or budget, as they represent the culmination of events and tasks leading up to a milestone. A milestone is marker of accomplishment. It might or might not coincide with a deliverable. Milestones are vital, particularly to project team members, because they offer a visible point of demarcation. They let team members know whether the project is proceeding according to plan. They represent a completion of sorts from which the project staff can gain new energy, focus, and direction for what comes next.

Keeping the Big Picture in Mind

In refining the WBS toward attaining its final form, it's useful to revisit the basic definition of a project as introduced in Chapter 3, "So, You're Going to Manage a Project?" A project is a venture undertaken to achieve a desired outcome, within a specific time frame and budget. The outcome can be precisely defined and quantified. By definition, the project itself is temporary in nature. It usually represents a unique activity to the host organization.

In many ways, the challenge of establishing an effective WBS is likened to meeting the challenge of various constraints. For example:

- Staff resources might be limited.
- The budget could be limited.
- Equipment and organizational resources might be limited.
- Crucial items on order might not arrive on time.
- Deliverables that you provide on time could be delayed by committees that have to follow various approval procedures.

Meanwhile, you have a project to lead and can't, or don't want to, spend the time waiting for committee members to respond. Even when deliverables are not the issue, you might encounter delays when you only need a simple *yes* or *no*. Key decision makers could be unreachable or too bogged down with other issues to respond to you in what you consider to be a timely manner.

What about when your project is delayed for days on end because some other project team has not conveyed a key deliverable to you? You might find yourself in a touchy situation. When progress on your project is dependent on the activities of other departments within your organization, or on the success and timely combination of some other project, frustration can mount!

What's potentially burdensome is that relying on outside approval or coordination can be difficult to plot on your WBS. As you assemble your plan, you have to account for delays in the time outside parties take to respond to you, even though they promised that such delays would not occur!

From a planning standpoint, if a group is supposed to respond to you in two days, you could consider their turnaround time to be four days. And, you might need to build into your plans a series of announcements and reminders focused on inducing them to respond. Perhaps a better alternative is to assess any risks associated with late responses or late performance, and then develop a contingency plan.

The Big Picture Versus Endless Minutiae

In your quest to assemble a comprehensive WBS, you run the risk of going too far. As stated in Chapter 5, "What Do You Want to Accomplish?," many a project manager has made the unfortunate error of mapping out too many tasks. When you subdivide tasks into too many subtasks, the WBS could become more restrictive or confusing than useful; this is analogous to government procurement specifications for acquiring a simple tool such a hammer or saw.

In assembling your project plan, avoid going overboard. Beware if you have hundreds of items listed for each event or task area, plus dozens and dozens of items scheduled each day for each staffer! Your quest is to maintain control of the project and have a *reasonable* idea of what each project team member is doing on any given day, but not venture so far as to become draconian. Some project managers have been accused, possibly unfairly, of charting bathroom breaks for staffers.

Micromanagement isn't pretty, particularly when you delve into the nitty-gritty of what responsible, competent project team members can handle. Moreover, micromanagers often focus on the wrong issues. The goal in constructing a suitable WBS and of being an effective project manager is to help your staff members achieve predetermined milestones in pursuit of an overall desired project outcome.

What number of subtasks in support of an event or task represents the optimal? Eight is probably too many and two is not enough. Someplace between three and five is probably optimal.

From Planning to Monitoring

Once the WBS is approved, your primary responsibility for the duration of the project becomes that of monitoring progress. This involves a variety of responsibilities:

- Keeping tabs on the progress, course, and direction of the project, noting any variation from the desired path.
- Modifying task descriptions when possibly needed as the project proceeds.
- Taking immediate corrective action if it appears that the project is veering off course, while continuing to adhere to overall schedules and budgets.
- Working with team members, enhancing their understanding of their respective roles, team building, offering praise and coaching, and incorporating their feedback.
- Controlling the scope of the project, which includes making sure that the desired levels of resources are expended on tasks and subtasks according to plan.
- While ensuring that roadblocks and barriers are effectively overcome and avoiding winning some battles at the cost of losing the war, sometimes you can expend too much effort in one area and leave yourself in a weakened position someplace else.
- Maintaining effective relationships with the authorizing party and stakeholders, keeping them informed, maintaining a "no surprises" type of approach, and incorporating their feedback.

Chapter 8, "Keeping Your Eye on the Budget," examines the need to carefully expend resources, including dealing with budgetary limits, equipment constraints, and other potential roadblocks. Thereafter, in Chapter 9, "Gantt Charts"; Chapter 10, "Critical Path Method"; Chapter 11, "Choosing Project Management Software"; and Chapter 12, "A Sampling of Popular Programs," we discuss how to manage more-involved projects.

QUICK RECAP

■ In assembling your WBS, there are several chicken-versus-egg issues that need to be resolved, such as whether to plot your own activities as a project manager and whether to include planning itself as a task.

■ Project managers have an easier time maintaining visibility of internal resources, including staff, equipment, and facilities, than they do when managing external resources, such as consultants, rented equipment, and leased facilities.

■ Your WBS needs to reflect realistic delays in receiving feedback from stakeholders following their reception of your scheduled deliverables.

■ Once you nail the WBS, you shift from a planning to a monitoring mode.

8

Keeping Your Eye on the Budget

In this chapter, you learn effective approaches to budgeting, how to combine top-down and bottom-up budgeting techniques, how optimism stands in the way of controlling expenses, and the importance of building in some slack.

Money Still Doesn't Grow on Trees

As project manager, a key responsibility of yours is to keep close reins on the budget. Your organization or whoever is funding the project enjoys hearing about cost overruns about as much as having a root canal.

Often the monetary resources allocated to a project (perhaps before you stepped aboard) have been underestimated. Why? Possibly as a result of exuberance the authorizing party or stakeholder might have had as to what can be achieved at what cost. This is not to say that project managers don't have their own hand in underestimating costs.

The project manager, nevertheless, often is charged with determining the project budget, as opposed to being handed some figure from above. In such cases, it might be useful to estimate a bit on the high side. This is true for a variety of reasons:

- In many organizations, no matter how much money you seek, you will not obtain it all. Ask for slightly more than your best calculations indicate, thereby increasing the probability of receiving close to the amount you actually seek.

- No matter how precise your calculations, how much leeway you allow, or what kind of contingencies you have considered, chances are your estimate might still be low. The proverbial Murphy's Law holds that if something can go wrong, it will go wrong. And Parkinson's Law contends that work expands so as to fill the time allotted for its completion.

- In ever-changing business, social, and technological environments, no one has a lock on the future even three months out, let alone three years out. You need to establish extra margins in your budget beyond those that initially seem commensurate with the overall level of work to be performed and outcome to be achieved.

So, is it foolhardy to prepare a budget that merely reflects the best computation as to what the sum *ought* to be? Probably. You likely need to ask for even more, and your project management experience, if any, plays a big part in your ability to discern the realistic monetary costs in conducting the project. A skilled laborer might be able to work wonders, for example, with less than top-of-the-line equipment. An entry-level laborer is likely to be less productive in the same situation.

Distorted Expectations

Ironically, the more competent you are as a project manager and as a career professional in general, the greater the tendency for you to *underestimate* the time necessary for project staff members to complete a job. You tend to envision the completion of a job through the eyes of your own level of competency.

"I have found through many years of experience," says one project manager, "that regardless of how competent the PM is or is not, there is a tendency to be overly optimistic on the estimated length of time need to complete a project. So, the smart thing to do is budget 15% to 20% more, because unforeseen issues arise." Even if you discount for newly hired and inexperienced staff, you will likely regard jobs in the way that you might have tackled them when you were newly hired. Thus, you underestimate the time required to complete the job with the staff you have.

The preceding phenomenon has a corollary in professional sports, particularly in NBA basketball. Many of the superstars who went on to become head coaches failed because they could not incorporate the lower competency levels of players on their current roster. Such coaches recalled their own playing days and what they achieved, and perhaps recalled super-competent teammates and competent players from other teams.

When coaching their current team, they can't shake their preconceived notions of what a player was supposed to be able to accomplish, the rate at which a player learned, and the skill level that the player could acquire.

Among any group of team members, of course, adjustments will be needed. As project manager, you might have vaulted expectations about how your staff are able to perform and what your staff can accomplish. You might eminently be more competent than they are on particular tasks. And, the opposite could be true! Members of your team could have abilities that exceed yours, in certain areas.

Whereas you might be the type of individual who moves through tasks rather quickly, others might be slower, or more unsure, or simply more cautious. You might be curious about a wide variety of issues, whereas a project team member might be more inclined to maintain solitary focus on the task at hand. The takeaway? Recognize that people on project teams, on a variety of fronts, rarely possess the same capabilities, work habits, or even inclinations as you or their colleagues do.

We are all imbued with our own talent and skills, as well as background, training, and education, not to mention energy level and enthusiasm. The ability to learn, to incorporate new instructions, or to adapt to changes on the fly could vary widely from team member to team member. The wise project manager recognizes this possibility, and proceeds accordingly when making schedules and when estimating the time and level of effort for tasks and activities.

Hidden Costs

An experienced project manager knows that when you rely on external sources to proceed on a project, such as subcontractors, hidden costs could emerge. If the subcontractor works for a flat fee or lump sum amount, it's easy to pinpoint that figure and plug it into the overall budget. What about *your* time and effort, however, or project team members' time and effort, in carefully preparing guidelines for subcontractors, working with them to ensure smooth operation, and consuming time in extra meetings, phone calls, and e-mails?

What about the extra reporting and other administrative tasks associated with working with outside vendors? Such factors ultimately affect the budget. The cumulative impact of underestimating time can quickly put your project in jeopardy. Even if you apply a safety margin to your estimate, the level of safety margin is applied through the eyes of your own personal competency. It's best to have help when preparing the budget, so consider a team approach.

Crises Will Happen

The experienced project manager expects that one or more crises will occur in the course of the project. The inexperienced project manager might be forewarned, but still is unprepared. Even experienced project managers know that sometimes you reach a point of desperation in the project—you have to have something done by a certain time and need to move heaven and earth to complete it.

You might have to pay exorbitant short-term costs to procure a vital resource, work around the clock, plead for added help, coax and persuade, or scramble like a rabbit in the brush to keep the project on time. Such encounters have a potentially dramatic effect on the budget.

Traditional Approaches to Budgeting

If you're managing a project that remotely resembles anything else anyone has managed in your organization, you'll want to seek any and all available insights on how to prepare a real-world budget for your project. Obviously, you don't want to merely lift the cost figures from one project and apply it to yours. Still, some cost elements of a previous project might be akin to some elements of your project, so you've got a good place to start.

Many industries have codified cost elements associated with various jobs. Printers have elaborate cost estimate sheets. Their estimators can plug in the particulars of a customer's request and quickly yield a cost estimate for the customer. With the many variables involved in estimating the cost of a printing job, however, the estimator can end up underestimating the true costs and, hence, diminish his profit.

In construction, for example, the cost estimator has comparable tools for that industry. The estimator might know the costs for each 2' by 4', brick, cinder block, and glass panel. By knowing the dimensions of the building, the number of floors, and the other attributes via project blueprints, to the best of his ability, the experienced estimator determines the overall cost of the construction project.

Nevertheless, you encounter stories about projects that ended up costing 50% or more of the original estimate, and about companies taking a bath on projects because the final costs were so out of whack with reality. Particularly on civil engineering projects, multimillion-dollar cost overruns make the daily news!

What's going on here? Why would experienced organizations that have performed hundreds of jobs for clients and customers, using sophisticated cost estimating software, be off the mark so often and sometimes so wildly? The skill of the person doing the budget estimate, the assumptions he or she relies on, and the approach he or she takes matters greatly. What's more, unforeseen factors often arise that add to the scope of work.

Traditional Measures

Let's discuss some traditional measures for preparing a budget, followed by a look at the cost estimation traps that are best avoided.

Top-Down Budgeting

Using this approach, a project manager surveys the authorizing party or committee, stakeholders, and certainly top and middle managers where relevant. The project manager also conducts a massive hunt for previous cost data on projects of a remotely similar nature, and then compiles the costs associated with each phase (if the project has phases), specific events or tasks, or even subtasks.

Borrowing from a bottom-up budgeting approach (see below), as a safeguard, the project manager might enroll project management staff, if they've been preidentified, and solicit their estimates of the time (and hence cost) for specific tasks and subtasks. The project manager would then refine his or her own estimates, which now could be somewhat higher than earlier estimates. In any case, the best estimate would be presented to the authorizing party.

Often, as emphasized earlier, the wise project manager lobbies for a somewhat larger budget than the authorizing party feels is necessary. Even if the project manager ends up yielding to the wishes of the authorizing party (which is predictable) and accepts a lower budget figure, safeguards have already been built into the top-down budgeting approach: The judgments of senior, top-level, highly experienced executives and managers likely already factor into budgetary safety margins and contingencies.

The project manager could possibly be the single project manager of many who are calling on the top manager or executive. Thus, the amount allocated for his or her budget could be in alignment and consistent with the overall needs of the department or entire organization. A persuasive project manager might be able to lobby for a bit more in funding unless there are extraordinary circumstances.

Bottom-Up Budgeting
As the name implies, this approach to budgeting takes the reverse course. After constructing the work breakdown structure (WBS), the project manager consults with project

staff members (again, presumably preidentified), who offer detailed, pinpointed estimates of the budget required for every task and subtask. The project manager would also routinely survey the staff once the project begins, to continue formulating the bottom-up budget, which is submitted to the higher-ups.

The project manager keeps an eye on cost trends—possibly on a daily basis, but more likely weekly or biweekly, and also in between one task and another. As project team members ascend the learning curve, they might attain operating efficiencies. More competent team members enable the overall project team to proceed on some aspects of the project with greater productivity and predictably lower costs.

This isn't to say that the project won't hit a snag or is otherwise immune to the potential cost overruns, as discussed throughout this chapter. The bottom-up budgeting approach offers great potential, along with significant risk. In their book *Project Management*, authors J. R. Meredith and Samuel Mantel state, "It is far more difficult to develop a complete list of tasks when constructing that list from the bottom up than from the top down."

While a reasonably accurate compilation of costs can be achieved using this method, if the project manager does not recognize all cost elements of the project, then the cost estimate can be off by a wide margin.

In addition, if project management staff suspects that top management seeks to cut budgets, then they might resort to overstating their case. This results in the project manager presenting a sum to the higher-ups that is larger than would otherwise be derived. Almost as in a chain reaction, the project budget might then be whittled away—a circular dilemma!

Still, as more and more organizations request that their staff people engage in project management as managers or team members, it makes sense to regularly solicit input from those who are actually doing the work. Frontline workers in any industry have a first-person, hands-on connection to what is occurring—whereas those not on the front line are comparatively distant observers often relying on compiled information.

When project staff is allowed to participate in preparing a budget, if that budget is cut, at least they had some role in the process, and, according to Meredith and Mantel, they "will accept the result with a minimum of grumbling. Involvement is also a good managerial training technique, giving junior managers valuable experience in budget preparation as well as the knowledge of the operations required to generate a budget."

Despite some wonderful potential benefits, most organizations and most projects do not rely on bottom-up budgeting. Top managers are reluctant to relinquish control of one of their chief sources of power—allocating monies—and sometimes mistrust subordinates, thinking that they might routinely overstate project needs.

Top-Down and Bottom-Up Budgeting

An effective approach combines the two budgeting techniques discussed above. *Top-Down and Bottom-Up Budgeting* involves gathering data and input from top executives, then soliciting input from project management team members and adjusting estimates accordingly.

Regardless of the approach, one needs to account for the disparity between actual hours on the job and actual hours worked. No project staff person working an eight-hour day offers eight hours of unwavering productivity. Breaks, time-outs, lapses, unwarranted phone calls, web searches, and "who knows what else" happen! As such, you might seek to apply a 10% to 15% increase in the estimates submitted by project management team members, especially in regard to the amount of time they'll need to accomplish tasks and sub-tasks.

If a task initially was determined to cost $1,000 (the worker's hourly rate times the number of hours), you would allocate $1,100 or $1,150 to better reflect the true costs to the organization. If you settle on the midpoint—perhaps the safest estimate—of your calculation, $1,125 dollars, you would plug that into the figures you present to top management.

Predictable Reverberations

During a project manager's quest to pinpoint accurate costs, bouncing back and forth between top management and team members happens. Depending on how your organization views project management and earlier established protocols, a constant flow of budgetary checks and balances might be the norm for how your project proceeds. Thereafter, budget approvals require a series of periodic authorizations.

Figure 10 shows one example of a project budget with actual and budgeted amounts recorded.

As involved as some project budgets that indicate both actual and budgeted amounts might become, keep in mind that project software programs (see Chapters 11 and 12) offer relatively easy-to-use, comprehensive budgeting calculation routines, spreadsheets, and other supporting tools.

Systematic Budgeting Problems

In assessing the potential costs associated with a task or sub-task, some costs might not be budgeted accurately. Suppose you're charged with managing a project to design a proprie-

FIGURE 10 Project Budgeting

Corporate-income statement	Actual	Budget
Revenue		
30 Management fees		
91 Prtnsp reimb—property mgmt	410.00 188.00	222.00 119.00
92 Prtnsp reimb—owner acquisition	.00 750.00–	750.00 .00
93 Prtnsp reimb—rehab	.00	.00
94 Other income	.00	.00
95 Reimbursements—others	.00	.00
Total revenue	410.00 562.00–	972.00 74.30
Operating expenses		
Payroll & P/R benefits		
11 Salaries	425.75 57.25	583.00 85.00
12 Payroll taxes	789.88 668.12	458.00 51.70
13 Group ins & med reimb	407.45 387.45–	40.00 135.30
15 Workmens compensation	43.04 .04–	43.00 100.00
16 Staff apartments	.00	.00
17 Bonus	.00	.00
Total payroll & P/R benefits	1668.12 457.88	1124.00 83.50

tary software system that could become a leading product for your company. Consider the following:

■ A variety of system development costs, including defining system requirements, designing the system, designing infrastructure, coding, unit testing,

networking, and integrating, will be involved, as
well as documentation, training materials, possibly
consulting costs, possibly licenses, and fees.

- Staff costs will accrue to identify, configure, and
  purchase hardware; to install it; and to maintain it.
  Staff costs could accrue to acquiring software.

- Staff travel, transportation, hotel and meal expenses,
  conference room and equipment fees, and perhaps
  costs for snacks and other refreshments could
  mount up.

- Costs involved in having top management, outside
  vendors, clients, and customers attend briefings need
  to be considered.

- Costs associated with testing and refinement, operations, maintenance, debugging, beta testing, surveying, and compiling data are likely.

What's more, little or no prior data might be available for
the project manager to use in estimating the cost of multifaceted projects. Equally vexing, budgets from prior projects
might confuse and complicate issues, rather than clarify and
simplify them.

Estimation Sand Traps

Sometimes, to put it bluntly, estimation sucks. Stay alert to
these estimation traps:

- Inexperienced estimators, especially those who
  don't follow any consistent methodology in preparing estimates, overlook some cost items entirely, or
  tend to be too optimistic about what is needed to
  execute the job.

- If you are managing a project that has a direct
  payoff for a specific client, your organization had

to bid tightly, perhaps too tightly, against considerable competition. Perhaps they low-balled to win
the contract, and your quest is to proceed within
these constraints, ever-seeking to trim costs each
step of the way—even when there is nothing left
to trim.

■ Sometimes organizations intentionally bid on projects they know will be money losers, hoping to
establish a relationship with the customer that will
lead to more-lucrative projects. This is little solace
for you if you have to grind out every ounce of
productivity from an already overworked project
staff, or by using plants and equipment to the max.

■ Careful and comprehensive project budgets could be
slashed by senior managers or executives who are
operating based on some agenda unknown to you.

In *The New Project Management*, author J. D. Frame
notes, "Political meddling in cost and schedule estimating is
an everyday occurrence in some organizations." The antidote
against such meddling, says Frame, is "The establishment of
objective, clearly defined procedures for project selection . . ."
which should be set up so that no one, "no matter how
powerful, can unilaterally impose their will on the selection
process."

■ ■ ■

The issues raised in this chapter point to the ever-present
need for project managers to build an appropriate degree of
leeway into their estimates. Rather than being dishonest or
disloyal to your organization, you are instead acknowledging a ruthless axiom of project management—that you
hardly ever obtain the funds you need, and even then, stuff
happens!

QUICK RECAP

- The monetary resources allocated to a project (perhaps even before you stepped aboard) frequently were underestimated.

- Often, no matter how much you seek, you can count on not obtaining it all.

- Although seldom employed together, the combined top-down and bottom-up approach to budgeting is quite effective.

- Build an appropriate degree of leeway into your estimates, or suffer!

9

Gantt Charts

In this chapter, you learn what a Gantt chart is, why it's valuable in project management, how Gantt charts keep your project on schedule, and variations of the chart that you can devise.

Chart Your Progress

Henry L. Gantt, for whom the Gantt chart is named, was an ordnance engineer during the First World War. He was employed at the Aberdeen Proving Grounds of the U.S. War Department (now the U.S. Department of Defense) in Aberdeen, Maryland. While a century has passed, Gantt's chart remains widely recognized as a fundamental, highly applicable tool for project managers everywhere.

Gantt charts are derived from your work breakdown structure (WBS). A Gantt chart enables you to easily view start and stop times for project tasks and subtasks. If you use an outline for your WBS, the Gantt depicts each of the tasks and subtasks in chronological order. For tasks that begin at the same time and run concurrently, the Gantt chart is a highly convenient tool. However, overlapping tasks and subtasks can easily be depicted on the Gantt chart, as well.

A WBS that is created from tree diagrams also lends itself to depiction on a Gantt chart, though the process is a bit tricky when it comes to determining overall project sequence as well as start and stop times. (Read more on converting tree diagrams to critical path analysis in Chapter 10, "Critical Path Method.")

A few basic forms of Gantt charts are depicted here:

1. The chart in Figure 11 uses bars extending from left to right along the horizontal axis to denote starting and ending times for events or activities. Greater detail could be added if you wish to add subtasks. Color-coding allows you to pinpoint which project workers are handling which tasks and subtasks. The chart offers a simple plan for depicting the planned sequence of events, even though obviously not everything will go according to plan, versus the actual (the shaded bars).

2. A Gantt chart with triangles, shown in Figure 12, is an alternative to the previous chart. Rather than using bars to depict start and stop times, and shaded

FIGURE 11 Gantt Chart with Bars

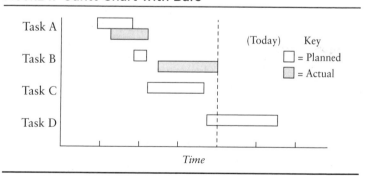

FIGURE 12 Gantt Chart with Triangles

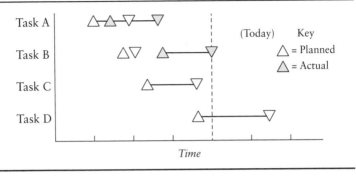

bars to depict actual performance versus planned performance, this chart uses:

- Unshaded triangles pointing up to depict planned start time
- Unshaded triangles pointing down to depict planned end time
- Shaded triangles pointing up to depict actual start time
- Shaded triangles pointing down to depict actual completion time

3. A Gantt chart with triangles offers other advantages. Tasks and subtasks, as well as planned versus actual time frames, can be depicted on a single line emanating from the left of the chart, extending out along the horizontal axis to the right.

The variations of the Gantt chart depicted in these figures (though there are many others) offer a snapshot of a project's progress based on time frames.

In Figure 11, though Task A didn't start on time, its duration was roughly equal to the original planned time. In Task B, however, the start time was not only delayed, but the actual completion time for the task was greater than originally planned. This could signal potential budget problems or human resource bottlenecks here or elsewhere as the project progresses.

If the start of Task C is not dependent on the results of Task B, then the manager can make a decision to initiate Task C as scheduled or even earlier, since delays in starting Task B might indicate the availability of idle resources.

If Task C is dependent on the completion of Task B, or at least most of it, then the project manager might have no alternative but to have Task C start late as well.

You can see that the delays in Tasks A and B could have a cascading effect that puts other project activities behind schedule, unless you as project manager can reallocate resources so as to maintain the pace when possible.

Variations on a Theme

Each of the three Gantt charts depicted thus far represents ways of illustrating overall project status while including the status of each task. Thus, they serve as valuable tools for keeping project team members as well as the authorizing party, committees, top managers and executives, and other stakeholders abreast of activities.

The Gantt chart in Figure 13, for a construction project, depicts an eight-week period that includes four items; three are actual tasks and one represents completion of the project. Each of the three tasks has between four and six subtasks. Virtually all project activity is dependent on maintaining the sequence of events as depicted.

The coding at the bottom of the chart indicates critical and noncritical progress, plus critical events. Scheduled start and stop times for the duration of tasks are earmarked by solid, downward-pointing triangles emanating from the start

FIGURE 13 **Gantt Chart with Sequential Construction**

ID	Name	January									February								
		2	5	8	11	14	17	20	23	26	29	1	4	7	10	13	16	19	22	25
10	Review current yard																		
20	Remove debris																		
30	Clear weeds, dead trees																		
40	Remove extra soil/cement																		
50	M: Basic yard cleared																		
60	Develop plan																		
70	2100 Select architect																		
80	Review yard																		
90	Develop plan																		
100	Present plan																		
110	Review plan																		
120	Revise plan																		
130	M: Plan approved																		
140	Install watering system																		
150	Select plumber																		
160	Develop plumbing plan																		
170	Review plan																		
180	Do plumbing																		
190	Review work																		
200	M: Plumbing complete																		

Critical	▬▬▬	Summary	▼▬▬▼
Noncritical	▬▬▬	Mgmt. Critical	▬▬▬
Progress	▬▬▬		
Milestone	◆		

and end of progress bars. Milestones are depicted by solid diamonds. More detail could be added in the form of other kinds of lines and symbols. The project manager devising this chart probably found this level of coding to be useful and convenient.

Embellishments Offer Detail

The more tasks involved in your project and the more important the sequence between tasks, the greater your propensity will be to embellish your Gantt chart. The chart in Figure 14 contains some added columns:

- Column 3, "duration," lists how many days each task is scheduled to take.
- Column 4, "predecessors," identifies what needs to be completed before this task can be initiated.

Often the previous task needs to be completed, but this isn't necessarily the case:

- For Task 7, "purchasing," both Tasks 5 and 6 need to be complete.
- For Tasks 8, 9, and 10, only Task 7 needs to be complete, as the other three tasks all start at the same time.
- For Task 12, "install software," Task 10 needs to be complete, but Task 11, which is scheduled to start after, does not.

You might wonder, "Why not switch Tasks 11 and 12 in the Gantt chart?" The answer is that Task 11, "develop

FIGURE 14 Gantt Chart with Multiple Predecessors

ID	Name	Duration (days)	Predecessors	Jan	Feb	Mar	Apr
21	Project mgmt.	4					
22	Needs analysis	11					
23	Specifications	7	22				
24	Select server	8	23				
25	Select software	14	23				
26	Select cables	5	24				
27	Purchasing	4	25, 26				
28	Manuals	15	7				
29	Wire offices	23	7				
30	Set up server	5	7				
31	Develop training	16	8				
32	Install software	5	10				
33	Connect network	5	9, 12				
34	Train users	10	11, 13				
35	Test/debug	15	13				
36	Acceptance	6	14, 15				

Critical ▬▬ Noncritical ▬▬

training," follows directly from the completion of Task 8, "manuals" whereas Task 12, "install software," directly follows from the completion of Task 10, "set up server." They are listed in sequence on the Gantt chart based on what they *follow*, not based on when they *start*.

One of the benefits of listing the task duration in days is that it also gives you a strong indicator of required levels of staff support. In the simplest example, if staff members have the same capability, and a 10-day project requires one staff person per day, you could add the total number of days in the duration column and attain a total number of staff days necessary for the project.

In the case above, leave yourself (as project manager) out of the duration computation, because you are fully involved in management and not engaged in any individual task.

The challenge grows more complex when two, three, four, or more staff people are needed per task for each day of a task's duration or, when varying numbers of staff people are needed per task, per day. It becomes further complicated if the skill levels of project staff vary widely. This is where Agile project management and scrum become useful. Sophisticated project management software and tools solve many issues related to multiple-resource complexity.

As I have emphasized throughout, *first* you need to understand the basics with paper and pencil, much like you had to learn the fundamentals of math on your own before being able to skillfully use a calculator.

Your Project, Back on Track

If you find yourself falling behind in one area, you have to make managerial decisions about keeping the overall project on track. These decisions will involve shuffling of resources, altering the scope of selected tasks or subtasks, or changing the sequence of tasks. Let's visit each of these:

- *Reallocating Resources*—It happens to the best of project managers: You launch into a task, and soon find yourself under-resourced. You didn't know that a particular task or subtask would prove to be so challenging! If it's critical to the overall project, borrow resources from other task areas.

- *Reducing the Level of Effort, or Scope, on Tasks or Subtasks*—While some tasks require greater staff resources, other tasks and subtasks might be completed with less effort than you originally budgeted. Perhaps some subtasks can be combined, or even skipped. If you're doing survey work, maybe you can still attain a quality result with, say, eight questions instead of 10, or can reduce the total number of interviews by 10%.

- *Altering the Task Sequence*—When faced with roadblocks, can you change the sequence of tasks or subtasks? Can you substitute easier tasks for more challenging ones until some of your other staff resources are free? Perhaps you can devise a sequence that enables some of your more experienced staff members to manage multiple tasks for a brief duration.

Thinking Ahead

The Gantt chart is also useful for engaging in "what-if?" questions. As you examine the sequence of events, their duration, and the number of allotted staff days, sometimes you see opportunities to make shifts in advance of the need. Such shifts might facilitate smoother operations down the road.

If you find that the first several tasks or subtasks on your project are already falling behind, a Gantt chart can help you identify where else this might occur, given your early operating experience. So, you could begin crafting possible scenarios using alternative Gantt charts that might be more effective for managing the duration of the project.

You could even have the pleasant experience of seeing tasks and subtasks completed in less time than you had originally plotted. If you do, use the Gantt chart to reschedule subsequent events, moving them up and taking advantage of the temporary gains that you've already realized.

■ ■ ■

In all, the ease of preparation, use, alteration, and sheer versatility of Gantt charts make them a marvelous tool for both managing your project and depicting your progress to others.

QUICK RECAP

- The Gantt chart is regarded as a basic, highly applicable tool that enables project managers to easily view start and stop times for project tasks and subtasks.

- The more tasks involved in your project and the more important the sequence between tasks, the greater your propensity and desire to purposefully embellish your Gantt chart.

- If you find that the first several tasks or subtasks on your project are already falling behind, a Gantt chart can help you identify where else this might occur, given your early operating experience.

- The Gantt chart helps answer "what-if?" questions when you see opportunities to make shifts.

10

Critical Path Method

In this chapter, you learn why projects become increasingly complex, the basics of the critical path method (CPM), and how to use that method to conserve resources.

Complexity Happens

Complexity happens more often than we care for it to occur. Suppose you're managing a two- or three-person team. With you and one other person, you have only one connection between the two of you. With a total of three people on a project you have three connections: one between you and person A, one between you and person B, and one between person A and B (see Figure 15). If only things stayed that simple!

With four people on a project there are six connections, and with five people there are 10 connections, as shown in Figure 16.

With six people on a project there are 15 interpersonal connections, and with seven on a project there are 21. Thus,

FIGURE 15 Two- and Three-Person Connections

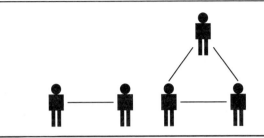

FIGURE 16 Four- and Five-Person Connections

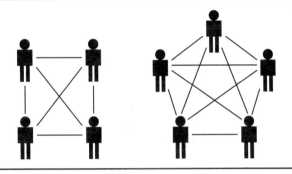

beyond five people on a project, the number of interconnections grows rapidly and can even become unwieldy.

Suppose that a vital item needs to be shared among your project staff. A *project constraint* is a critical project element such as money, time, tools, human resources, or something else that is, or becomes, in short supply. Then, add some other resource constraints such as when project team members can use a particular piece of equipment and when that equipment needs to be maintained: a constraint. What if the equipment is unavailable due to repair time: possibly a major constraint!

Now, add a second needed resource, such as access to a database, or reliance on a survey in process, or another piece of equipment. With many people on your project team, and with time, money, or resource constraints, effective management becomes complicated.

Add some tasks that are dependent on the completion of previous tasks and you have the recipe for bottlenecks, roadblocks, and, potentially, project inefficiencies. Complexity, as project resources grow, is not necessarily anyone's fault; rather, it is often the result of restraints, interconnectedness, and dependencies.

The Gantt chart, discussed in Chapter 9, "Gantt Charts," is a valuable tool, particularly for projects with few project team members, the project end approaching, and relatively few project constraints. For larger, longer-term projects involving many people, resources, and constraints, project managers need more sophisticated tools for maintaining control.

Enter the CPM and PERT

The critical path method (CPM) was developed in 1957 by Dupont Incorporated. Even if you personally do not have to engage in CPM analysis, it makes sense to know the fundamentals. CPM in a project is the path that takes the longest to complete. By definition, the critical path has no slack. If you fall behind along the critical path, the entire project falls behind schedule.

A second project management technique, whose approach is somewhat like CPM but more involved, is the program evaluation and review technique (PERT). PERT was developed in 1958 by Booz-Allan Hamilton and the Lockheed Corporation, in participation with the U.S. Navy, on their joint Polaris submarine-launched nuclear missile project. It offers a degree of control that becomes essential for many projects, especially large ones, perhaps those larger than you as the typical reader of this book can likely manage.

Using PERT, a project manager will seek to identify a task or set of tasks that represent a defined sequence crucial to project success. A PERT chart, in its true sense, depicts a three-point approach to estimating possible duration times for tasks, typically categorized as *optimistic, likely,* and *pessimistic.* Estimating in this way enables project managers to gain a stronger grasp of how the project schedule might realistically unfold.

CPM, which we will explore in the balance of this chapter, is a useful approach to project management because it enables a project manager to monitor the impact of various project developments. For example:

- If a critical task slips by a few days and ends up starting at the same time as a succeeding critical task was originally scheduled to start, what takes precedence? With two critical tasks, the one that starts late *has to be completed before the other starts.*

- What happens by keeping project staff on one task for an extra three days? If the task is on the critical path, it will delay the other critical tasks by, you guessed it, three days.

- What is the impact if a noncritical task slips by two weeks? It depends on how much float that noncritical task has. If it has, say, 16 days of float, then two days of float would remain.

To emphasize: A critical task refers to a single task along a critical path. A noncritical task refers to a task within a CPM network for which slack time is available. Slack time is the time interval when there's leeway as to when a certain task needs to be completed.

Great Utility

Project managers have used CPM to compress project schedules by identifying which tasks can be undertaken in parallel—a valuable capability—when initially it might have appeared that they needed to be undertaken sequentially.

Since the critical path represents that path that takes the most time to complete, it contains no slack. Delays along the critical path affect the entire project, whereas tasks not on the critical path have some slack in their completion time. So, team members assigned to noncritical path tasks might not have to work quite as steadfastly as those assigned to critical path tasks. If they're not careful, however, their total duration can exceed that of the critical path. As such, they could cause the project to fall behind schedule, as well.

Keeping in mind that this book is titled *Everyday Project Management,* is of moderate length, and is not a 480-page tome, let's observe step by step how you can use CPM to manage a simple project. We'll keep it to two people on this project: you and a friend. With 10 events or tasks, including a start and an end, only nine tasks actually require attention.

1. Create a work breakdown structure for the project. Figure 17 serves as our example, with duration times listed in minutes.

   In this example, the path requiring the most time is Task 10, the 40-minute drive to the outing site.

2. Using the information in the WBS, create a flowchart like that depicted in Figure 18. Notice that in this flowchart some tasks can occur simultaneously. Bill's tasks are depicted above, and Erika's tasks are depicted below.

   Dark or fine lines indicate the relationships between the boxes. For example, "prepare sandwiches"

FIGURE 17 **Work Breakdown Structure for an Outing**

Task	Duration (min.)	
Start	6	
Make drinks	30	Bill
Prepare sandwiches	20	Erika
Prepare fruit	4	Erika
Prepare basket	4	Erika
Gather blankets	4	Bill
Gather sports gear	6	Erika
Load car	8	Bill
Get gas	12	Bill
Drive to outing	40	Erika
End	0	

FIGURE 18 **CPM Network**

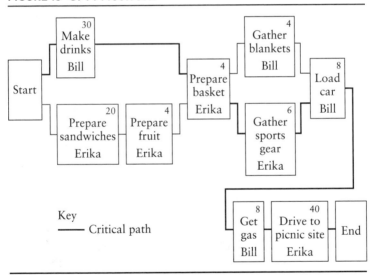

and "prepare fruit" are connected by a thin line. Bill's task "make drinks" connects to Erika's task "prepare basket" with a thick line, which we'll address shortly.

Both Bill's and Erika's tasks lead to "gather sports gear."

3. Because "make drinks" requires 30 minutes and Erika's tasks consume 20 minutes and 4 minutes respectively, "make drinks" represents the critical path in this project, indicated by the black line between Bill's first and second activity.

Erika's path has six minutes of slack. If she starts a few minutes late or lingers for one or two minutes between tasks, as long as her total slack doesn't exceed six minutes she'll still finish before Bill. Conceivably, she could take her time on each task, adding a minute or two to each and still finish before Bill. But if her slack equals six minutes, she'll finish at the same time as Bill.

4. The critical path for the entire project as depicted above can be traced by

   ■ Identifying which tasks occur simultaneously.
   ■ Noting which ones take longer.
   ■ Routing the critical path through them.
   ■ Summing the entire length of the critical path.

   In the preceding case, the entire project would require 100 minutes. It sounds straightforward so far, doesn't it?

5. So, putting our knowledge to use: For this or any other type of project, examine the earliest times that critical tasks need to start. Then determine the earliest times that noncritical tasks could start. Column 2 of Figure 19 indicates the earliest start times for Bill's and Erika's individual as well as combined tasks.

   Column 3 shows the late start times for Tasks 2, 3, and 5, the first two tasks handled by Erika, and the latter handled by Bill. The total slack time—the

FIGURE 19 **Roster of Events with Early, Late, and Slack Time**

Task	Early start	Late start	Slack
1. Make drinks	0	0	0
2. Prepare sandwiches	0	6	6
3. Prepare fruit	20	26	6
4. Prepare basket	30	30	0
5. Gather blankets	34	36	2
6. Gather sports gear	34	34	0
7. Load car	40	40	0
8. Get gas	48	48	0
9. Drive to outing	60	60	0

cumulative sum of time that various tasks can be delayed without delaying the completion of a project—for Tasks 2, 3, and 5 respectively are six, six, and two minutes, as depicted in column 4.

In calculating the latest acceptable start times, work from right to left. Focusing on the critical path, if the overall project requires 100 minutes, the latest start time for the last task ("drive to outing") occurs at the 60th minute. This is derived by subtracting 40 minutes of driving from 100 total project minutes.

Similarly, "load car" and "get gas" need to commence by the 40th and 48th minutes, respectively. The drive begins at the 60th minute and the service station stop lasts for 12 minutes. Hence, 60–12 = 48. The other values can be computed likewise.

6. The computation to determine the latest acceptable start times for noncritical times also proceeds from right to left, like that described above. Slack time is computed by subtracting the earliest determined start times from the latest possible start times. Said alternatively, subtract the values in column 2 from

the values in column 3, and the resulting value in column 4 represents your slack time.

Slack time occurs when both project team members are simultaneously engaged in individual projects. When both work on the same project, there is no slack time—and joint project activities lie on the critical path.

What If Things Change?

By chance, if Bill finishes Task 2, "make drinks," in less than 30 minutes and Erika has done her job as scheduled, up to six minutes could be reduced on the overall project critical path. If Erika starts at the earliest times indicated, works diligently, and finishes at the 24th minute mark as originally planned, she could possibly help with some of Bill's subtasks that lead to the successful completion of Task 2. His help might save a few minutes off the total project time.

The reverse could also occur. Attempting to help Bill, Erika might spill something, mix the wrong ingredient, or otherwise cause a delay. If so, you would add back minutes to the critical path determination equal to the length of the delay that she caused.

Because the task durations represent estimates, and few tasks might proceed according to plan, the overall project time could vary widely from what Bill and Erika first estimated. They might save one to two minutes on Tasks 5, 8, and 9. Meanwhile, a traffic back-up on this fine Saturday morning could turn a 40-minute trip into 50 minutes.

Time saved here and there often lags time lost. On many projects, some tasks invariably thwart the project manager and require 20% to 50% more time than projected. The project manager who has consulted with others (see Chapter 6, "Laying Out Your Plan," and Chapter 7, "Assembling Your Plan") and has engaged in both top-down and bottom-up planning perhaps can avoid such wide variances, but not always.

I Feel the Need, the Need for Speed

Along the critical path, adding more resources to the mix could shorten the overall time frame. If a friend helps Bill and Erika load up the car, a minute could be saved. This is not a dramatic example, but consider the impact of having one person help another move from one apartment to another. The addition of a second worker yields considerable time savings, especially in lifting bulky or heavy items that one person could not easily handle.

When additional resources are allocated for a particular task, this is called *crashing*, an odd name for a beneficial development. Crash time represents the least amount of time to accomplish a task or subtask with unlimited resources, such as all the equipment or all the funds you desire.

In *Project Management*, authors Meredith and Mantel estimate that on real-world projects, less than 10% of the total activities actually represent critical activities. Yet, examples of CPM often depict projects in which critical activities outnumber or outweigh noncritical ones!

Most tasks have several subtasks associated with them. So, our CPM network depiction offers only a broad-brush view of a rather simple project. Examining Task 1 further, suppose that one of the subtasks involved is to add sugar. As Bill mixes up the drinks he adds a tablespoon of sugar and then he takes a drink. Is it sweet enough? His subjective answer will be *yes* or *no*.

If he concludes "not sweet enough," then he has a new subtask: adding more sugar. He repeats the taste test and eventually concludes that the level of sweetness is on the mark. Only then does he pack up the drinks. This activity can be depicted by the flowchart in Figure 20.

FIGURE 20 Flowchart of "Make drinks" Task

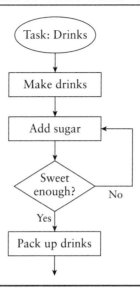

If we incorporate the simple loop that we've created in this "make drinks" flowchart into the overall CPM chart depicted in Figure 18, we would have additional boxes, with additional lines, plus additional arrows emanating from Task 1, "Make drinks," thus complicating our chart.

Likewise, other tasks could include associated subtasks which involve *yes* and *no* questions, and repeat loops, until a condition is satisfied. Repeat loops add more delays and increase the complexity of a CPM analysis.

Let's Network

Expanding on the chart in the CPM network in Figure 18, a depiction of tasks and subtasks is called a *network diagram,* or *configuration,* or simply a *network* for short. Available project software tools greatly assist in this area.

When manually constructing the network for simple projects and concurrently enhancing your understanding of critical path charts, you'd sketch and resketch the network until you thought you had it right. Then you would bounce this off team members, challenge everybody's assumptions, and ensure that you had not overlooked any tasks or sub-tasks that were vital to the project.

A link that indicates an association or relationship between two otherwise parallel tasks along a CPM network is called a *dummy* task or activity. Seasoned network diagrammers sometimes add a dummy activity that reveals the relationship between two events, even though no tasks are actually performed. Project management software enables you to apply many other charting options, and some can be quite handy.

Me and My Arrow

The *activity-on-arrow* CPM network is a useful variation to the chart depicting the CPM network and is shown in Figure 21.

FIGURE 21 Activity-on-arrow CPM network

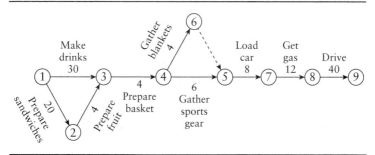

Notice that the critical path line here is constant, starting from Task 1, proceeding to Task 9, while noncritical activities represent diversions off the critical path. Tasks are represented by the bars with arrows. (Thus, they're called "activity-on-arrow.") Events that represent the start or end of a task are depicted by circled numbers.

Gathering blankets, Task 6, leads to Event 6, which then is connected by a dummy task, as already described. This is depicted in the figure as an arrow with a broken line leading to Event 5. Of the two possible diagrams for CPM networks, either will suffice—it's a personal preference.

Manually updating a CPM network when changes become evident, or when the estimated duration of a task needs to be altered, can be a true pain. With software, though, the updating is instantaneous, much like updating a cash flow analysis using spreadsheet software: You update some figures and, presto change-o, the monthly cash totals and even the year-end cash total change instantly to reflect the latest updates. With CPM, as you introduce new data into the system, a new critical path configuration immediately appears on your screen.

Don't Fall in Love with the Technology

Mastery of charting processes can lead to problems, especially among technically oriented project managers. Project managers have been known to become enamored of technology. The tools at their disposal can seem intoxicating, if not addictive. Some project managers become overly smitten with the charts and printouts at the cost of

- Effective communication with stakeholders.
- Managing the project team.
- Serving as a liaison to top managers, executives, and stakeholders in general.
- Meeting the needs of the customer, who likely requires interim psychological stroking.
- Ensuring that the final desired outcome will be achieved.

Tellingly, many studies of managed projects reveal that the most frequent causes of failure are *nontechnical*, such as the lack of commitment among project team members, hidden political or personal agendas, or the project manager's inability to effectively communicate project results (the subject of Chapter 13, "Reporting Results").

■ ■ ■

Employ work breakdown structures, Gantt charts, CPM, and the software packages about to be discussed, for they all have great worth. Keep your eye on the people-related dynamics of the project, however, since managing people well is the primary make-or-break factor for success.

QUICK RECAP

- Managing a project of five people is considerably more complex than managing a project involving only three. With each new person, or each new resource, many more lines of connectivity occur.

- Any given project follows a critical path, and a delay in any activity along that path delays the overall project.

- "Crashing" a project means allocating additional resources to a particular task, usually to complete it in less time than originally allotted.

- It's easy to fall in love with the available charts and project management tools, though project failures are often actually a result of neglecting the human dynamic.

11

Choosing Project Management Software

In this chapter, you learn the types of software programs that are available, their capabilities, and which software functions are crucial, and you are given some guidelines for selection.

With the Click of a Mouse

Project management software (PM software) is available at a variety of prices, offering a wide variety of functions. You can use software to plan, initiate, track, and monitor your progress. You can develop reports, print individual charts, and at the touch of a screen (or a click of a mouse) e-mail virtually any aspect of your project plans to any team member, top manager, executive, or other stakeholder.

Many earlier versions of PM software focused on planning, scheduling, and results. Tools for communicating, analyzing your progress, finding critical paths, and asking "what-if?" questions were sometimes lacking, depending on whose software you employed. Today, there are many options among a multitude of vendors.

Also, until recently, for many projects, word processing, database, and spreadsheet software was often used instead of project management software. Of note:

- While fewer people used PM software previously, project participants and stakeholders usually did see the generated output.
- PM software quickly took hold because it enabled more customization than many other types of software.
- PM software tended to be more expensive than commonly used software, but the costs were offset by gains in productivity and in managerial effectiveness.

Leave a Good Thing Alone

In the past few decades, project management software went from being expensive and crude to less expensive and highly functional, then to even less expensive, but sometimes confusing. When *Harvard Project Manager* was launched in 1983, it represented a breakthrough in PM software. Its main focus was on project budgeting, scheduling, and resource management.

With *Harvard Project Manager* you could generate Gantt charts, PERT charts, and CPM charts, plus a variety of other charts and tables. It was considered an integrated project planning and control package and sold for as little as 30% of the price of its less functional predecessors.

Three decades later, competition among PM software vendors heated up, prices came down, and functionality went sky high. While some packages can be hard to learn, many are relatively easy to learn. Consider your own experience in using word processing or graphics software. Aren't there earlier versions of current programs that were easier and more convenient? You were able to install and learn them in days, and go on your merry way.

With today's software, if you are starting from square one, you might have to attend a training session. If you have a flair for software, perhaps you can be up and running quickly. Vendors embracing Agile or otherwise tend to include everything, plus the kitchen sink. This gives them the opportunity to design splashy ads listing umpteen features and to charge high prices. Realistically, how many people are true power users who would use most of the advertised features?

Whose Choice and Whose Job Is It?

If your organization or department already uses or prefers a certain type of software, then your decision, understandably, is already made. Your quest becomes mastering that software—or at least the parts critical for you to know. The upside is that if a brand of PM software is the preferred choice in your workplace, and other projects employ such software, you are fortunate: Other project managers or staff will know how to use it and can serve as ad-hoc software gurus to you.

When there are no experienced users in your work setting, and you have options, which kind of software might you choose? In general, select a popular and well-known package. The price is likely to be competitive, stakeholders likely will have heard of the vendor or the software, and you won't have to vigorously defend your decision to higher-ups.

If you and you alone will have responsibility for learning the software, you need to build in the time and add in the expense to your budget, for it will take you time to learn it or to take a course, and your time is costly.

While it seems obvious that you as the project manager are likely to be the primary user of PM software, please rethink that assumption. Depending on what you are managing and the dynamics of your organization, if you are the primary software user, you might spend the brunt of your time working with the software, with precious little time left for forming and building your team, maintaining reporting requirements, and offering the day-to-day level of project management that the venture requires.

Recognizing the danger of having a project manager become too immersed with PM software, some organizations have established support groups or even provide internal software gurus, especially for larger projects. These gurus serve as in-house experts and can be lent to project management teams for the duration of the project.

The gurus work directly with project managers, incorporating their feedback, answering questions, and undertaking whatever types of analysis the project manager requests. They routinely maintain schedules, budget various reports, and track the allocation of resources. An experienced software guru knows how and how often to share project-related reports with project staff and project stakeholders.

What's Your Pleasure?

Assuming that your organization will *not* be lending someone to you who'll handle the brunt of PM software activities, and assuming no particular program of choice has been established, how do you go about selecting software? Begin by acknowledging what kind of user you're going to be, which is largely determined by two elements: the size of your project and how technical you are.

For small projects of a few months or less with zero-to-two staff, it's possible that no project management software is necessary! How so? You might already possess the software and software knowledge you need to be effective in managing a small project. We're talking about the aforementioned spreadsheets, word processing programs, a graphics or drawing program, and the functionality to generate tables, graphs, flowcharts, and other diagrams.

Though somewhat makeshift, the combination of reports and exhibits that you can muster with your current software and skills might be suitable for your project needs. Your current software could be entirely adequate if the basic work breakdown structure (WBS) and a Gantt chart or two are all you require and if you don't necessarily have to create a critical path.

For projects involving four or more people, extending several months or longer, with a variety of critical resources, it makes sense to invest in some type of software, even if it isn't necessarily PM software per se. Many calendar and scheduling software programs come with built-in functions. They let you produce tables, devise Gantt charts, and even maintain a schedule for four to 10 people. Nevertheless, all things considered, with at least four people, on a project lasting several months, procuring some dedicated PM software makes good sense.

The Project Management Institute at www.pmi.org and the Project Management Control Tower at www.4pm.com each offer a variety of books, audiovisual materials, training guides, classroom training, seminars, and online training. The website www.ProjectManager.com offers a host of career opportunities for project managers and those seeking to enter the profession, as well as books, guides, and audiovisual tools.

Dedicated PM Software

Inexpensive PM software is your best option if you don't have anyone else in the organization who can serve as guru, and also when you wish to automate rather than manually generate critical reports and charts. Or, if you're managing many people over many months, and have 1,000+ tasks and subtasks to complete, you'd seek PM software for midrange project managers.

The competition among dedicated PM software vendors embracing Agile, or not, is keen. Notable suppliers include Workfront, Primavera, Mavenlink, Basecamp, Asana, Easy Projects, and Trello. (See Chapter 12, "A Sampling of Popular Programs," for an overview of PM software.) Lower-end programs such as TeamGantt, Project Kickstart, and Milestone Simplicity can also help you generate plans, project reports, and basic charts, and they don't require significant learning time. They are both affordable and easily downloadable, instantly.

You can spend anywhere from $200 to $6,000 using the more feature-laden versions of software named above. Such packages will give you the full range of tools sought by even veteran project managers on multiyear projects.

High-end project management software is designed for the longest duration, largest, and most involved types of projects. Yet, if you are a high-end user, you wouldn't have picked up this book! Here, we are talking about software that can range from a few thousand to many thousands of dollars. Learning such packages could take weeks. Even at the high end, so many programs are available that you might need a consultant to make such a selection, and the process could take weeks or months.

Regardless of your level of PM software knowledge, your selection might prove to be a key factor in overall project success. Alas, many project managers find that the software they chose (and purchased!) is too complex and too unwieldy to use for the entire project. Some end up using only an element of the software, such as budgeting or scheduling; some use it only for making charts; others may end up abandoning the software midstream. In such cases, a lot of scrambling follows because whatever the software was used for now needs to be done manually.

Will you decide to schedule and track subtasks and tasks based on identified start times and stop times for each staff member, all the time? Or will you rely on your staff to give you estimates of task and subtask completion times?

- Relying on the input of your staff helps to build a team, but it takes more work.
- Using the software is arduous at first, saves time later, and keeps you in front of a screen more often—perhaps away from the people and events occurring around you.

How Will You Use PM Software?

The first time, modest users obviously won't use PM software the way that an experienced pro will. As such, several usage options are worth considering:

- *Reporting*—Here the project manager uses the software to generate Gantt or possibly CPM charts. The PM might use other software programs such as word processing and spreadsheets to supplement the project graphs and produce reports.
- *Project Tracking*—This refers to a system for identifying and documenting progress performance for effective review and dissemination to others.

Project tracking software is used to compare actual versus planned progress. As the project staff completes tasks and subtasks, the results of their efforts are logged so that the tracking effort stays current.

■ *What-if Analysis*—The PM software is engaged to identify the impact of changing the order of subtasks, shuffling resources, or changing tasks' dependencies. "What-if?" analysis is invariably satisfying, because you attain immediate feedback. One caution: If you change one variable at a time, you gain a good grasp of the impact. If you change too many variables at once, the picture can become cloudy, diminishing your ability to gauge cause and effect.

■ *Cost Control*—Project managers use PM software to allocate costs to various project resources. This is usually done by figuring out how much resource time and effort are consumed. Be careful that the cost computations you make will plug niftily into the overall cost structures of your organization's accountants.

■ *Clocking*—By regularly updating project team member hours expended on various tasks and subtasks, project managers can generate reports indicating actual versus scheduled use of resources.

Checklists and Choices

While it can be difficult to generalize about which type of software various levels of users might require, here are some general criteria worth considering:

■ Ease of use—Is the software easy to install, with good help screens, tutorials, and customer support? Is the software menu-driven and intuitive? Is it easy to move items around? Are the commands standard and easy to learn? Is the manual or instruction guide easy to use? Are you able to start quickly?

■ Reporting functions—Does the program allow for individual revising of report formats? Can these be easily imported into other software programs? Can they easily be saved, added to, combined, and read?

■ Charting capacity—Are options easy to use? What about drag-and-drop capabilities? Can charts be imported and exported easily? Are supporting graphics easy to see and to use? Can charts readily be changed into other forms?

■ Calendar generators—Does the software allow for calendars of varying durations, in a variety of formats, for different aspects of the project and project staff, with the ability to mark particular days and times, including holidays and other nonworking days? Are these calendars also easily importable and exportable?

■ Interfacing—Communication functions with those both near and far are valued features of project management software. Can you easily connect with remote staff, and are data easily shared with others who require online access? Is the software efficient in terms of byte space consumed?

■ Report generation—Can a variety of report formats be selected, with quick changing capabilities as well as easy transference to word processing software?

In addition, consider these attributes in the software you're considering:

■ Shows onscreen previews of reports prior to printing
■ Offers a variety of formats for Gantt and PERT charts

- Works with a variety of printers and other equipment
- Enables several projects to share a common pool of resources
- Conveys cost data by task or by time
- Allows printing of subsections of charts
- Accepts both manual and automatic schedule updates

Most of the systems you encounter, fortunately, offer such capabilities. So, go beyond a strict comparison of software functionality and consider the attributes, benefits, and services of using a particular vendor, as well. For any major purchase it's advisable to have a good set of questions. The following is a list I've used in several of my books. Ask the vendors whether they

- Offer any corporate, government, association, military, or educator discounts
- Have weekly, monthly, or quarterly seasonal discounts
- Offer off-peak discounts
- Guarantee the lowest price
- Issue a money-back guarantee, or other guarantees
- Have guaranteed shipping dates
- Staff a toll-free customer service line, and help via online chat functions
- Avoid selling, renting, or otherwise using your name and ordering information
- Insure shipments
- Charge for shipping and handling
- Include tax and any other charges
- Provide demos available for free
- Feature free or low-cost upgrades

- Have references available, especially a list of satisfied customers in your area
- Have been in business long

Making a List, Checking It Twice

After you've established your selection criteria, in acknowledgment of everything that your project entails, and in consideration of the various attributes, benefits, and features of working with each vendor, here is a useful exercise:

Decide on paper what you *must* have versus what is *nice* to have versus what is not needed, but you'll take it if offered. Then, using product reviews, critical articles, and the vendors' own websites, make a preliminary survey of the available packages and how they stack up. A matrix or grid with the vendors listed across the top representing columns, and the attributes vital to you on the left side of the page, will suffice.

You might encounter 10 or 12 possible vendors, but seek to reduce the list early to three to five. Virtually all vendors have online product demos. If possible, observe the software in use either in your own organization or elsewhere. Observing software in use is revealing! You glean far richer information than from a website or, for that matter, a product demo. Someone in the field, using the software, can provide first-person input as to where the software shines or seems kind of dim.

Some vendors allow you to download a full package to use for a limited duration. Sometimes, a particular feature is so outstanding that it outweighs other mediocre elements of a vendor's overall package.

In summary, if you've narrowed the field to a few vendors, you have a decent chance of identifying the one that best meets your needs!

QUICK RECAP

- PM software has lately become much more sophisticated and more bewildering. Many packages can aptly handle the jobs that you need to do, but might be difficult to learn, let alone to master.

- Many organizations loan software gurus to a project or have other project managers who can supply ad hoc mentoring. If this applies to you, you are fortunate.

- Don't become so immersed in software that you lose contact with your project team and the environment that surrounds you.

- Choosing appropriate software is vital. Predetermine your selection criteria so that you're not buffeted by an endless array of options, benefits, and features.

12

A Sampling of Popular Programs

In this chapter, you learn which software programs are popular, what vendors have to say about their own programs, and the importance of taking your time when acquiring software.

Swiftly Flow the Days

With each passing day, any software program evaluation presented in any book or magazine ages and soon becomes obsolete. Consequently, the surveys and reviews of products listed in this chapter are presented for the sake of example only!

A survey titled "Tools of the Trade: A Survey of Project Management Tools" appeared years back in an issue of the *Project Management Journal*. The journal evaluated what the authors called "Top Project Management Tools." Some 159 project managers responded to survey questions out of 1,000 managers initially contacted. The typical respondent had slightly more than 10 years' project management experience and a bit more than 12 years' experience in the field of information systems. In other words, this was a select group of veteran project managers.

The 159 respondents cited *79 different project management tools* that they either were using currently or had used within three years. Of note, the top 10 of these 79 tools were identified by three-quarters of the respondents. The tools were rated for their content, accuracy, format, ease of use, time lines, and then given an overall rating.

Not surprisingly, the training time that project managers received for the various software packages (which they *had* to learn) influenced how adequate they thought the software to be. Said alternatively, the more training you have to work with a particular type of project management software, the higher you tend to rate that software. So, familiarity (and training) does not breed contempt and more likely yields satisfaction.

Armed and Online

Flash forward to today: The array of software options available is even more bewildering than that of years ago. And, since virtually all project management tools have an online component, the power and capability of such programs are truly awesome. Project management teams today, across the globe, rely on software to stay in touch, manage workflow, work in harmony with one another, and bring part of a project in on time, on budget, and at the desired quality.

The top project management software packages enable project managers to automate workflows so that when one project task or event is completed, everyone is informed and any recalculations to the critical path or need for reassignments are derived almost automatically.

It's accurate to say that there is a huge range of effective software, depending on the size of your organization, how much you are willing to pay, how experienced your users might be, what you're trying to accomplish, the length of the project, and so forth. The permutations and variations are enormous.

As you read through descriptions of the various types of available software programs presented below, keep in mind the common denominators among each of them. These include the ability to engage in "what-if?" scenarios, seamlessly connect with team members, enable people to make their own updates, and generate timely and relevant reports that can be presented to stakeholders.

When assessing any other software programs you might encounter, it's useful to read up on what experts say about them, as well as to talk to people in the field who actually use them. That said, descriptions of six different packages follow. One or more of them might be perfect for you! Following that is a discussion of three bargain-basement packages, which, in themselves, might do the job that you need.

Also, as years pass, most companies will still be in business and the software will change, perhaps from version "2.0" to "3.0." From that standpoint, it makes sense to peruse the various components and features of the software, while recognizing that it's always subject to upgrading. Indeed, any vendor is likely to update what they regard to be their own "effective" software within the course of a single year.

Workfront Project Management System

Big-name companies such as Dell, Cisco, Sony, REI, and others are devoted users of Workfront, an online project management system designed to improve a company's processes as well as its return on investment. Workfront is especially useful with information technology teams and project management offices, known as PMOs.

Workfront provides a roster of traditional project management supports and methodologies, as well as options for sideways communication. This is where, in addition to offering a top-down approach to project management, the software also supports peer-to-peer collaboration, offering social media–like tools that facilitate transparent communications. Sideways communication also encompasses interaction with both internal staff and external stakeholders.

With Workfront you can rapidly create projects on the fly, drawing on existing templates or even previous projects. Projects can also be devised based on requests from management, peers, or deliverables recipients and other end-users.

As you read the rest of the longish Workfront summary, keep in mind that other project management software vendors described after Workfront also offer varying arrays of more or less similar benefits and features.

Drag-and-Drop Capabilities—Workfront enables a project manager to plan projects, devise schedules, schedule milestones and deliverables, allocate resources, generate Gantt charts, update schedules, and enable team members across time zones to interact effectively. It assists in identifying resources based on availability, type of skill, or other details. Project managers can "drag-and-drop" assignments on their computer screens between project team members and then can quickly affirm what has been assigned to whom.

Workfront equips the project manager with control tools, such as granting team member access to specific data. You can create profiles that enable others to have access or not, and to address specific areas of the system. You can devise complex passwords using a sign-on technology tool, and can specifically block a user from seeing, for example, sensitive financial information.

On the accounting side, Workfront can generate budgetary tracking and financial reports that can be exported to accounting systems. Any particular report can be reconfigured to highlight potential problem areas, and to help keep projects, as well as individual tasks, on track. Customized fields can be easily added to monitor specific information and run reports off such customized fields.

Keeping Tabs—Workfront enables you to establish specific viewing screens for project directors or other stakeholders, and lets such parties assist in making project decisions, without burdening them with an overabundance of project details. A roster of built-in reports helps project managers succeed with deliverables while gaining "lessons learned" during the execution of the project. The system also offers alerts to approaching milestones and events.

The manufacturer contends that Workfront scores the highest both among their own project testers and among team members at actual user sites. It's been reported that the common and routine staff member tasks can be initiated without extensive training. In other words, the software is intuitive and straightforward.

Another advertised Workfront feature is that basic project management functions, such as adding tasks, updating budget information, adding resources, and monitoring workflows, are simple to accomplish. Workfront customers say they routinely experience gains in productivity, on-time delivery, and the ease with which they accomplish other tasks.

Workfront integrates well with Microsoft's Outlook e-mail program and other collaboration and document management tools, and can share data via Google Docs, SharePoint, and Dropbox, and also with sales/marketing systems such as Salesforce, Jira, and ExactTarget.

Supporting Services—After you purchase the software, Workfront professional staff will perform a variety of training and hand-holding functions, help you undertake periodic checkups, and tweak your system for optimized performance. Users are connected with a single service representative as point of contact, who both manages your account and connects you with other Workfront support staff as required. Workfront support is a mandatory aspect of employing the system for Year One and can be a bit costly, but it generally proves to be worth the outlay by helping ensure your optimal use of the system and achievement of your goals.

Asana

Another software application, Asana, is a task management program geared to producing effective project management on the team level, enabling users to sync between computers and mobile devices, while integrating with third-party programs to yield a versatile viable system. Its advertising slogan is "run your day, your team, and your company."

Asana offers a system in which several projects can be established, tracked, and managed. Similar to big-ticket project management software packages, Asana enables you to establish a comprehensive task list, organize tasks in a variety of ways, establish due dates, and assign staff responsibilities.

Because it is a cloud-based system, permitting users to manage major projects or individual tasks, it aids both companies and their teams assigned to handle multiple projects at one time. Specific features include a dashboard, collaboration tools, automatic notifications, task management, reporting, document management, customer portals, and an inbox feature that automatically updates and informs participants as data is generated and new input is applied.

It's a popular program for a variety of reasons: You can create projects and tasks within projects and can track the progress from the various browsers and devices. You can easily modify existing projects and tasks, as well as share files and communicate with project staff. Asana can be accessed through a variety of devices including smartphones, laptops, and tablets, and can be accessed on both iOS smart phones and Android phones.

Asana offers a smart inbox and can be integrated with Google Drive, Dropbox, Slack, Harvest, Sunrise, MailChimp, WordPress, and HipChat, offering up to a 100 MB limit per attachment. It has a system, called the smart inbox, for refining what arrives in a team member's inbox. Instead of weeding through unwanted or insignificant messages, team members see what is important quickly and easily. Once it's installed, you don't need outside e-mail or specialized apps for communications or organization of messages.

For large teams, one of Asana's top benefits is vanquishing difficulties that large teams encounter as they attempt to maintain cohesiveness. Asana is adept at enabling project team members to manage their work load, prioritize tasks, and organize tasks as necessary, as well as delegate duties, upload files, and make reports.

Asana's e-mail capability, as well as its instant messaging function, allows team members to review and discuss project progress as it unfolds, to share information, comment on it, and attach or upload a file as needed. In addition, key conversations can be saved on team pages so that other team members can benefit from the innovative observations and solutions that are generated.

As with major software packages, when a change is made on a project or task, team members can receive immediate notifications and are invited to note, "like," follow, or comment on the update. Asana enables one team member to cite another in the comments section to ensure that that person is in the loop, much like Facebook enables you to tag your friends.

Asana's success is partly a result of its ability to streamline complex workflows with project team members, even among large tasks. You can tag individual tasks to later find them quickly and conveniently. With relative simplicity, Asana is employed to create, categorize, and schedule projects, and enables individual users to track projects to completion.

A listing of Asana features includes

- Real-time updates
- Project contacts creation
- Comments on tasks
- Tracking tasks
- Custom calendars
- Automatic updates
- Activity feed
- Notifications and reminders
- Multiple workstations
- Mobile device support
- Setting goals, priorities, and due dates
- Gantt charts

Mavenlink

Another program, Mavenlink, offers key features beyond project coordination, communication, and updating. With Mavenlink users can generate a variety of different reports, record billable hours, and create charts on the fly that help you to see the big picture of where the project is heading. The more complex your project, the more you might prefer software like Mavenlink, which is adept at handling staff assignments, shipping deadlines, and outside contracted assistance.

At the start of a project, as the project staff is assembled, with Mavenlink you can enable specific individuals to have access and permissions to specialized data and information. Project staff can record their own progress, attach or upload files, and communicate freely on project-related issues.

As with other software described in this chapter, Mavenlink provides considerable flexibility. You can easily add custom fields, including client contact information and subcontractor information. An indexing capability allows you to search by project team member name, message, or other selected topics. Mavenlink also is compatible with other key business programs, including Salesforce, QuickBooks, and Microsoft Office.

The software has embedded critical-path-tested capabilities. For example, you have a task that has to be completed within 10 days, but another task can't start until the first task is finished. With Mavenlink you are immediately alerted as to when to start the second task. Mavenlink also enables you to organize, store, and share any file related to your project, and maintains them in one convenient place. Likewise, it has a straightforward, easy-to-access platform to help manage all project activities and individual team member activities.

Mavenlink enables an organization of any size to adroitly manage the entire lifecycle of a project, as well as project-based relationships. This includes interactions between a project manager and team members, financial reporting, file management, communications and messaging, invoices, and vendor payments.

Mavenlink's cross-platform collaboration feature makes it easy to receive project updates as they happen, post information, share information, and keep in touch with team members, on the same page, in a way that is simple for people to access.

A sampling of Mavenlink capabilities includes

- Project and job costing
- Personnel planning
- Task dependencies
- File sharing
- Team collaboration
- Project summaries
- Invoicing
- Expense tracking
- SSL (Secure Sockets Layer) security
- E-mail integration

In considering if Mavenlink might be right for you, contemplate whether you'll take advantage of the advanced tools it offers, which large organizations and seasoned project managers find highly useful. If you need a less sophisticated, simpler, and intuitive type of software with basic features, you don't need Mavenlink.

Basecamp

An online project management suite, Basecamp, lets you set it up easily, learn it on the fly, and initiate a project the same morning. It helps to organize clutter and chaos resulting from the efforts to successfully manage a multifaceted project that includes a large number of tasks and subtasks, as well as work done by project management staff. When projects end, it offers a quick summary of accomplishments in report form and can generate automated reports to share with stakeholders.

Basecamp has been described as "covering a lot of bases," notably in managing both projects and project staff with team members scattered across the country or around the globe. Basecamp claims to be the first software that introduced remote project management, and has improved this capability with each new software release. Because it is entirely cloud-hosted and provided as a service, users do need to take on a variety of updating and maintenance chores. Pay a monthly fee, and Basecamp's systems software engineers handle all matters related to software performance.

One of its key benefits is enabling you to devise project templates to accomplish a specific task, track your progress, and modify or reuse assets as desired. As with other major software programs, you can add tasks with a few mouse clicks, assign them to project staff, establish a deadline, set up communication channels with discussion capabilities, add task notes, and send and receive files via e-mail or a mobile device. Basecamp works with both Android and iOS operating phone systems, and it syncs with a variety of apps, making it quite versatile.

With Basecamp you can manage from your smartphone. It offers a high-function dashboard on the homepage, which enables you to view multiple projects that are being tracked, mark them, and highlight which ones presently require your attention. Twenty different apps embedded in Basecamp aid you in accomplishing a variety of objectives while using your phone, desktop, or laptop.

Basecamp is less viable for traditional project management planning and control, while being more adept at assisting with team member to-do lists, file sharing, calendar management, and keeping abreast of chosen priorities and actionable items. It helps you to manage files associated with mid- to large-size projects productively.

The manufacturer cites one million+ users and says the basic software has been popular for longer than a decade. Some of the line-item benefits and features are

- Document management
- Project templates
- Scheduling
- Task histories
- Set priorities
- Add recurring tasks
- To-do list management
- Creating teams or groups
- Social collaboration platform
- Interactive Gantt charts
- Instant messaging
- Overall scheduling
- Real-time chat
- File storage

Basecamp appears to be a viable program for sharing ideas among teammates, perfecting proposals, and organizing the conversations. You can prioritize the order of tasks as desired and can tailor and tinker with the system to meet your specific needs.

Easy Projects

One straightforward, moderately priced project management system is called Easy Projects. It's used by higher education groups and sales and marketing organizations such as Ernst & Young, United Parcel Service, and Symantec.

Boasting a long list of customers around the globe, the software comes in many languages, including Spanish, German, Russian, and French. It is geared for those who've been thrust into project management and don't necessarily have a command of industry jargon or of the conventional tools.

Among Easy Projects' benefits are an exceedingly large amount of storage space, unlimited custom fields, and the ability to include guest users without limits. Basic functions such as adding and scheduling resources, injecting comments, and even creating new projects are all relatively simple. The terminology and icons employed are intuitive, making first-time project managers feel more at ease. The manufacturer claims its objective in creating the application was to devise software that virtually anyone can use, independent of one's background and training.

Unlike many of its project management software competitors, this software enables you to run payroll reports. Reports can also be displayed in a wide variety of formats. Project team members can readily submit their time logs based on a built-in timer, by single entry, or via manual submission.

The software's calendar function can be filtered by project name, customer, date, or custom criteria and can be used for team functions as well as individual workloads. If a project manager prefers, easy projects can be configured so that he or she receives a notification when critical events occur, or, if preferred, can be informed in an e-mail digest. Thus, managers can gain updates as to what is occurring even by the minute.

Conception and Creation—Easy Projects offers a variety of planning tools for conceiving and creating projects. Once a user starts to build a project, even first-time managers are pleased to find that they can do so with relative ease. The software can create bar charts, pie charts, and tables, as well as generate reports as PDF documents or as Excel spreadsheets. In terms of reporting, Easy Projects offers options, including more than 30 preconfigured report formats that users can employ or further customize.

Flexibility is the name of the game with Easy Projects, as it supports as many as eight kinds of custom fields, enabling a user to readily track, if desired, custom data which then can be assembled in report form and/or used for tracking purposes.

The ability to easily drag and drop Gantt charts enables you to modify schedules, track tasks, alter dependencies, and schedule resources. The project planning tools available to users, besides traditional Gantt charts, include resource load simulators that enable managers to engage in "what-if?" type queries.

All-in-All—While it's easy for first-time managers to use, the software does *not* support traditional methodologies such as Agile, critical path, or Waterfall. The help guide requires a bit of upfront navigation, but once you arrive at the desired section, the supporting text is helpful. Another concern: When adding time expended on a specific task, initially it takes longer to determine how to add it. Once handled, it isn't difficult.

As with virtually all the major software packages available, the vendor provides both product and project management training and follows up with implementation services. A certain level of training is regarded as mandatory for long-term success. Easy Projects' active social media adds a layer of peer support that many users find helpful. The manufacturer continually updates and makes accessible a healthy volume of free training materials and, in general, seeks to create long-term partnerships as opposed to simply gain more customers.

Trello

Unlike many leading project management packages, Trello employs what are called "concept boards," each of which corresponds to a project. Within each board, "cards" are analogous to individual tasks and enable you to track project progress or simply categorize items and maintain control.

Trello facilitates the ability of stakeholders—called "members"—to discuss projects or tasks in real time, helping them and project staff stay informed through a variety of methods. Because it is a collaborative system, members of a collaboration can receive e-mail notifications, updates of activity logs, and even updates of task assignments. Any particular member can be added to a board (again, this corresponds to a project) where the member may vote on ideas related to the cards (which represent tasks).

Trello's card system includes all the possible bits of information about a project. Some of Trello's benefits and features are

- Activity logs
- Assigned tasks
- Information retrieval
- Information backup
- Search function
- Text and visuals to fit any screen size
- SSL encryption of data
- Developer API
- Mobile access to boards

Trello gives you a choice of three packages. The *free package* enables you to have unlimited boards, cards, member checklists, and attachments, all of which means it will probably be sufficiently flexible for many users. The free plan enables you to integrate with Dropbox, Drive, and Box, and to include file attachments and correspondences of up to 10 MB.

Contrast the above with the *business class plan,* which includes everything in the free version of Trello, plus integration with Google Hangouts, Mailchimp, Google Drive, Dropbox, Evernote, Github, Slack, and Salesforce. File attachments of up to 250 MB are included. A Trello feature called *collections* enables you to organize all your team boards and to maintain control with quick and convenient one-click access. Removing former members is equally convenient.

Trello project managers have the ability to act as gatekeepers, granting who can create public or private boards. Likewise, company information can be kept private with access granted by having selected membership invitations. Business class users who run into trouble are afforded quick turnaround e-mail support with a key contact person and are offered a one-day guaranteed response time during business hours.

Trello's third plan, for vigorous users, includes all the features of the business class plus robust security protocols. One can stay in touch with an account executive to facilitate training or simply to maintain high productivity over the course of a project or even in the middle of the day. This third plan also enables project team members to be accorded seamless access to the parts of the system for which they have been approved.

Low-Cost Options

If you prefer to spend next to nothing and still obtain software to manage your project, many low- to no-cost programs are available, three of which are cited here. Depending on the size of your project, its duration, and other factors, any of the following might work well.

TeamGantt

Could Henry L. Gantt have possibly known in 1915 that software would be named for him? TeamGantt, project management software based in the cloud, obviously emphasizes the use of Gantt charts in managed projects. The overarching concept is that charts make it easy for people to understand lots of data all at once. Gantt charts are especially easy to design, complete, update, and share as needed.

TeamGantt enables you to quickly devise a variety of Gantt charts, based on your needs. For example, the chart called "project creation and task management" allows you to display several projects in a single chart, view them in multiple ways, and quickly pinpoint those with overlapping time lines.

Tasks can be tracked based on percentage of completion and be color-coded for easy viewing. Project team members and others such as stakeholders can make comments and submit them to other participants. The software records and saves all such comments and organizes them as conversation threads.

Charts from finished projects can serve as a template for the next project, certainly a handy feature when you seek to create common or recurring tasks. The software also can save "project views"—snapshots of the project or components of it—as well as the task status associated with it. Such viewing enables managers to instantly note the latest changes and how that affects overall project progress.

Concerned about team Colaboration? TeamGantt enables users to easily collaborate by sharing charts with one another. Participants stay "up to speed" by logging in and viewing the latest posts and progress.

TeamGantt pricing comes in three plans: a free version, the standard version, and the advanced version. The software can be accessed via desktop computers and laptops using Windows, and also via iPhones and Androids.

Features of TeamGantt include

- Project management
- Task management
- Conversations
- Employee monitoring and management
- Project visualization
- Access on the go
- Printed PDF files
- A variety of reports
- Subgroup access

Project Kickstart

Sometimes project managers are not sure what they want in their plan. Project Kickstart aids in generating ideas by asking key questions, offering specific guidance as needed, and allowing users to rapidly devise an effective, organized plan that includes project phases, interim goals, known obstacles, and viable solutions.

Project Kickstart helps managers to identify problems, contemplate potential remedies, and create an organized, streamlined framework. From this framework, the project plan and schedule automatically update, based on new input related to tasks, milestones and deliverables dates, or other changes.

As with TeamGantt, Project Kickstart offers numerous professionally designed Gantt charts that allow you to establish dependencies between tasks and to view automatic updates as the changes are applied. The software's "intuitive" capabilities help you to quickly generate PowerPoint presentations derived from various aspects of the project. It also offers "what-if?" type of queries to assess the impact of changing task parameters or resources.

The vendor emphasizes that effective project management requires having a good understanding of one's resources, being organized, paying attention to detail, and keeping track of the budget. Project Kickstart links easily with Microsoft's Word, Outlook, and Excel, as well as with MindManager, Act!, WBS Chart, and Mindjet. It helps you to effectively, yet rapidly, organize your notes via a straightforward user interface; assists in keeping projects on track through basic budgeting, milestone tracking, and cost tracking; and also monitors the percentage of tasks or subtasks completed.

Project Kickstart provides no-cost sample projects that include such plan elements as tasks, subtasks, goals, and obstacles. Thus, you can get a hands-on feel for how to manage your project before ever entering your own data.

Milestone Planner

A project management and business planning application called Milestone Planner gives users the ability to track which project management staffers are tasked to do what, and by when. This low-cost project management software, in one survey, had a notably high user satisfaction rate of 95%.

With Milestone Planner you can assign tasks, devise milestones, and track progress using your web browser and are supported by such features as (in the vendor's terminology) *work streams, goals, actions,* and *milestones.* You can integrate the software with a desktop calendar and, if desired, can sign in using e-mail, Twitter, Google, or a browser ID.

Milestone planner is geared toward coordinating "distributed teams." It helps users to collaborate in real time while allowing them to make notes and comments, record milestones as they are reached, and make other updates. All other participants can keep track of such changes and generate their own reports.

As with other software described in this chapter, Milestone Planner enables you to produce a snapshot of project progress in general, or by selected areas, and to produce high-quality charts, documents, and slide presentations.

With Milestone Planner you can add new team members and other system users as you desire, via customized e-mail invitations, with a 30-second sign-up process. The milestone planning function offers dynamic calendars that conform to the iCalendar standard and are supported by leading desktop calendar applications such as IBM Lotus, Microsoft Outlook, and Mozilla Sunbird, as well as Apple iCal, letting users stay abreast of project progress as new data is updated.

Milestone Planner tracks the changes made during the project's lifetime. Thus, users can track progress and see who made updates and changes, and when they did so. Histories of milestone achievement and of the entire project are readily accessible. Milestone Planner features include

- Plan templates
- Mobile interface
- Data export
- Time line review
- Change tracking
- Activity stream
- Microblogging

- SSL encryption
- A variety of action lists

The standard edition of Milestone Planner is free. The professional edition is offered at a low monthly cost and includes unlimited guest invites, templates, searching, reporting, calendar synchronization, and RSS feeds.

Other Resources

Don't overlook various PM software available via free trials online. It can be helpful to test them and get a feel for how such software works. Some PM software online is completely free, while offering less functionality than the for-fee version. Still, free versions could well be suitable for what you need. Also, many people already have some version of Microsoft Office Suite, which includes project management software. This might be adequate for your needs.

No Perfect Matches

Depending on the size of your organization and what you seek to accomplish, you'll likely have some unique requirements and perhaps unique desires. No particular software application will perfectly match your specifications. The quest for a perfect off-the-shelf project management software system is illusory. However, it's likely that you can find a system that will meet most of your needs and will prove to be quite helpful.

Online interactive search tools, such as those at www.capterra.com, can help you narrow the search. If you type "project management software" into its search engine, you are quickly shown that there are 700+ software options. This might seem overwhelming, but the options are broken down further into *project management*, *construction management*, and *project portfolio management*.

By clicking on *project management*, you can narrow the search even further, and then make selections based on whether software incorporates Agile methodologies, includes Gantt charts, offers customizable templates, and so on. Eventually, you can narrow down your selection to a handful of prime software candidates. Then you need to closely assess the few remaining software candidates as to how they fit your particular needs, the skill levels of your team members, your budget, and other constraints.

■ ■ ■

Caution is advisable: Take your time rather than hurriedly jump into acquiring software applications, even if they have proven to be highly beneficial for others. Conduct your own research, assemble relevant reviews, call vendors, talk to users in the field, and then seek the plan that comes closest to what you need.

QUICK RECAP

- PM software changes so rapidly that books aren't published fast enough to review the latest version of the top software.

- The more training that project managers have with a particular type of PM software, the more highly they rate that software. Hence, training is vital for multiple reasons.

- Virtually all vendors offer online project management capabilities, plus software support. With the complexity of the programs they sell, support could be crucial!

- No particular software application is likely to perfectly match your specifications.

- Take your time rather than hurriedly jumping into acquiring highly promoted, leading applications, even if they have proven to be supremely beneficial for others.

13

Reporting Results

In this chapter, you learn about potential difficulties in reporting your results, how to effectively use communication tools and techniques, the value of giving credit to your team, and the importance of assuming any blame alone.

More Communications Channels, Less Accessibility

In this age of sophisticated software (as described in the previous chapter), not to mention the web, smart phones, and whatever else becomes available, it should be easier than before to communicate your progress as you proceed on your project. Yet, for some project managers the experience is the opposite.

The increasing number of communication vehicles have resulted in making it more difficult to capture the time and attention of those to whom you need to report, even when they are waiting for your report! Does this seem like a paradox?

Many communication vehicles mustered considerable impact, for a while, following their widespread acceptance in the marketplace. Thirty to 40 years ago, it was a big deal to receive a FedEx package. Today, when express packages from any vendor arrive, sometimes they merely add to the burden of what you've already received that morning via other information and communication vehicles.

At least several times during the week, many people in the workforce feel inundated by too much information—if not each day and much of the time. Are you among them? Think back to yesteryear, when today's communication devices were not available. How did the typical project manager convey reports to his or her boss? Chances are the two worked literally within shouting distance of each other.

Is it any wonder, then, that project managers have a more difficult time reporting results at scheduled intervals, not to mention at random times, throughout the course of their projects? The ability to e-mail a skillfully developed WBS, Gantt chart, or CPM chart offers no guarantee that the recipient will review them as scheduled—or at all!

Starting with the least technical, least involved method of communication—one person talking to another—let's proceed through widely available communication options at your disposal, with an eye on how to employ them to your best advantage.

In-Person Communications

For scheduled meetings where you have to report your progress, the key word is preparation. Align your ducks. Have your charts completed, assemble your notes in order, and devise bullet points of what you want to present. The person to whom you are reporting is ultra busy. This project could be one of many items or concerns that he or she needs to monitor.

If your face-to-face report is to a committee, preparation becomes even more important. Committees are more critical and less accommodating than a single person. If you're using presentation software, *restrain* yourself! It's too easy to go on and on, showing slide after slide in brilliant color, with words that shake and sounds that go boom. Such features extend the length of your presentation and tend to take you off the mark of what you need to be reporting:

- If you have a video to present, make it six minutes or less. Three minutes or less would not be too short, depending on your project, your current progress, to whom you report, and other dynamics of your organization and the situation. Brevity is the soul of wit when it comes to making an audiovisual presentation!
- Whether you're using a flip chart, wall chart, chalk board, white board, or presentation hardware, prepare in advance. For flip charts and wallboards, map out and complete what you can before the presentation begins.
- For white boards and other media that you add to on the run, work from comprehensive notes and schematics prepared in advance so that you don't meander.

Informal Person-to-Person Meetings

For informal, person-to-person meetings, employ the same guidelines. Be brief, be concise, and be gone! Catch people when they are seated, when they can click a mouse, take notes, or staple something together. When someone is standing, follow-up and feedback activities aren't nearly as viable unless they have their cell phone out and are ready to record or take notes.

Don't collar anyone in the lunchroom, the hallway, the lavatory, or anywhere else unless you've established prior protocols for such interaction.

If you're asked to informally say a few words in a group meeting, stand and face the entire group while they are sitting. Independent of what you say, standing will convey more authority. Again, be as concise and brief as practical. Be open to insights and constructive criticism. Thank the group for their attention and depart gracefully.

Telephone Contact

Perhaps your project responsibilities include phoning your boss several times a day, once daily, several times a week, once weekly, or only occasionally. Regardless, seek to schedule your key phone calls; otherwise, you're likely to end up with voice mail, a result that can be frustrating if you need an interactive conversation then and there. As you have experienced, the likelihood of actually reaching someone you have called at random is declining.

With luck, you will each respect each other's needs to be not unduly interrupted during the day. Texting is useful in situations where immediate feedback is crucial but a phone call might be impractical.

If you happen to end up with voice mail and talking to a machine, here are some guidelines for being effective in that circumstance:

- Aim for a message between 35 and 55 seconds long. Too short, and the other party is likely to discount the importance of your message—unless, of course, it's something like "Leave the building! It's about to blow!"

- Longer than 55 to 60 seconds, your message might raise the ire of the other person, who undoubtedly has been receiving messages from other people all day long.
- Speak precisely, whereas others often speak hurriedly. If you know that you've reached a landline, offer your phone number at a speed that actually can be written down by the respondent on the first listening. A good way to approach this is to pretend that you're writing your phone number in the air with your finger as you announce it over the phone.
- Offer something compelling in your message. Saying, "Please call me back," is not nearly as effective as, "We need your answer on how to handle the extra shipment."

E-mail

If you think a face-to-face report or a phone conversation is warranted, you're probably right. Follow through. If you need a "Yes" or "No" answer to a project-related question and have leeway as to when you might receive the answer, e-mail is a great tool. If you need to easily transmit a report or data to others waiting for it, as you know, e-mail can also be highly convenient.

Here is a brief roster of appropriate project reporting uses of e-mail:

- Approval or disapproval
- Forwarding vital information to appropriate parties
- Data, charts, summaries, estimates, and outlines requested by recipients

At times e-mail can be inappropriate for reporting purposes, such as conveying:

- Overly complex topics
- Outlandish, highly novel, or earthshaking ideas
- Items requiring major discussion, clarification, or delicacy
- Emotionally charged information
- A hard copy paper trail is necessary or helpful

Dr. Jaclyn Kostner, an expert on e-communications, says that e-mail is better than voice mail when

- A written record is needed.
- The team's normal business hours in each location are not a match.
- You've been unable to reach the person interactively, but know the person needs the details.
- Language is a barrier. In multilingual teams, written words are frequently easier to understand than spoken ones, especially when accents are heavy or language skills are less than fluent.

Conversely, leave a voice mail or answering machine message when

- The sound of your voice is key to understanding your message.
- The recipient is mobile. In that case, voice mail and texts are easier to access than e-mail.
- Your message is urgent.

Memos and Informal Notes

These days, a hard-copy note sometimes commands more attention than texting, voice mail, and e-mail. Don't underestimate the impact of a handwritten, brief, friendly note such as, "Making good progress on Task 2, anticipate completion by tomorrow afternoon and smooth transition to start Task 3."

If you choose to write by hand, use your best handwriting. It is of no value if your handwriting looks like a flea fell into an inkwell, climbed out, and then staggered across the page before dying. Poor penmanship can cost businesses millions of dollars as a result of misunderstandings, disconnections, rewrites, and revisions.

Formally Composed Documents

Whether you type and then print a letter to be hand-delivered, sent by fax (some places still use fax), sent by mail, or delivered by courier, proofread your own document. Proofread especially if the document is a *deliverable*. The document likely will make the rounds and eventually will be viewed by stakeholders. Any typo or grammatical error that you haven't corrected, even if tiny and not crucial to the overall understanding of the document, tends to diminish your status.

As with person-to-person meetings, keep your document focused—short is better than long, and concise is better than rambling. Offer all your contact information on any document that you submit to project stakeholders, including your name, address, phone, e-mail, cell phone, and whatever other electronic leashes ensnare you.

Teleconferencing

Teleconferencing could occur between you, your project staff, and those to whom you are reporting, or it could be you alone reporting to others. Teleconferences often are conducted in conjunction with online presentation materials. For example, the committee hearing your report can follow your slide show in the sequence that you're presenting your material. This can be done by uploading your presentation to the host location in advance and simply referring to each slide as numbers 1, 2, and so forth.

Your recipients listen, you hope, on some type of commercial speakerphone. Hence, your words need to be as clear and succinct as you can offer. Slow your pace a bit and ensure that words and sentences have clear endings. Some words sometimes are not clear; some words on speakerphone, despite the claims of manufacturers, seem to sound clipped. Even sophisticated speakerphones designed for top executives at teleconferences might have shortcomings. A small degree of channel noise might be evident, though this is diminishing as newer and newer models appear.

As you likely know, a variety of Internet vendors such GoToMeeting, Zoom Video Webinar, or Webex can assist in facilitating the transaction in real time. Whichever way you proceed, don't employ your cell phone's speakerphone capabilities. It could sound like you're in a tin can or at the bottom of a well. Pick up the phone and speak into the receiver or use a headset, available in office supply stores. Have your notes sequentially laid out in front of you, to offer a logical, easy-to-understand telephonic presentation.

Be prepared for the same round of observations, insights, and criticisms that you might experience in person. Teleconferencing participants are less likely to speak up than they would be in person, but the potential is still there.

Web-Based Presentations

Depending on the dynamics of your situation, you might be able to fulfill the formal aspects of your reporting requirements via web pages and certainly using the communication and data-sharing capabilities built into the various PM software programs. The watchword here is effectiveness. Don't splash lavish colors plus audio and visual effects onto a presentation that distracts from your overall message rather than enhances it.

The beauty of big computer screens on office desks is that the charts and slides that you send will look as magnificent on their end as they are on yours.

Oh, Them Golden Bullets

Could you possibly overdo it when it comes to disseminating messages, data, and information? In *Project Management for the 21st Century*, authors Bennett Lientz and Kathryn Rea observe that "messages are golden bullets—you use them sparingly." Some project managers overcommunicate. They spend too much time with verbiage and too little time addressing the issue at hand. Before preparing a report or delivering a presentation to any project stakeholders, consider the following:

- Will the information have strong impact, and what will be its aftereffects? Will someone misinterpret what you have offered? Have you been as clear as you can be?

- Contemplate in advance who receives your message: both those present when you first delivered it, and anyone else who will encounter it later.

- To the degree that you have leverage, decide on the best medium to deliver your message and the best timing.

- Stick within established boundaries. If your report is supposed to be three pages or less, keep it to three. If it is supposed to be delivered via attachment, make it happen. If it is supposed to be free of graphics, keep it free of graphics.

■ Seek feedback. What value is it to you if you deliver a report and don't receive a timely response? You might head in a slightly different direction because you didn't attain the needed input in a reasonably timely manner.

Incorporate the Thoughts of Others

It is often to your advantage to emphasize "we," not "me." When preparing a report to others, either in person or via cyberspace, in real time or delayed, if practical incorporate others' opinions and ideas into what you're doing. For example, you could say, "As José suggested to us the other day, we chose to proceed with XYZ. This turned out well for all involved."

If practical, relate within your report how you are progressing and how your work might benefit the organization as a whole. Accent the milestones that you've achieved and the deliverables you've offered, while not going overboard. Share the credit and praise for a job well done, with as many people as you can. Bring credit to your team even if you did the brunt of the work. Upper management tends to know what's going on regardless. The upshot is that you'll look like a team player; someone worthy of promotion.

Conversely, accept blame for what didn't go so well without casting aspersions. You will appear to be a "stand-up" guy or gal, and people tend to have an unvoiced appreciation for this.

■　■　■

Be honest when it comes to addressing your own performance. Some leeway is permissible for tooting your own horn, *if* it is an accurate toot. No one likes a braggart or a report filled with fluff. No one likes to be deceived. Stay on the up-and-up, and develop your reputation as a project manager with integrity.

QUICK RECAP

- The increasing number of communication options can actually make it more difficult to grab the attention of those with whom you correspond and those to whom you must report.

- For scheduled presentations of any variety, the key word is *preparation*.

- A hard-copy note can generate more notice these days than voice mail or e-mail.

- Incorporate the words of others and give credit to the group, but personally accept blame.

- Be entirely honest when it comes to addressing your own performance.

14

Multiple Bosses and Multiple Projects, and Staying Balanced

In this chapter, you learn how to keep your wits on multiple projects, help your bosses not to overload you, handle multiple reporting structures, and be assertive when overload seems unavoidable.

Multiple Projects at a Time

Sometimes you're asked to manage this and manage that. Organizations will often assign smaller projects to up-and-coming managers, such as *you*, as a form of on-the-job training. By enabling you to try your hand on small fleeting projects, this will make you better prepared to tackle larger ones. Some companies also assign newly hired staff to serve as project team members on small projects, so that they will gain a wider view of company operations and, in time, can manage some of the smaller projects themselves, on their path to leading larger ones.

Managing small projects—even one-person projects—requires many of the same skills and essential elements found in the largest of projects. As you'll see in Chapter 16, "Learning from Your Experience," the skills that you acquire, and the insights and experience you gain, represent grist for the mill.

By its nature, project management tends to be a short-term, challenging endeavor. The opportunity to tackle small projects, and even a series of small projects simultaneously, invariably is a worthwhile career challenge.

Attitude Adjustment—Reframe your focus about participating in or managing multiple projects *as opportunities worth mastering.* As you hone your planning, monitoring, and organizational skills, you become a more valuable employee to your organization. Undoubtedly it has launched previous projects where managers failed to achieve the desired outcome. Either budgets were overrun, time frames were missed by a mile, morale dropped to zero, or chaos ruled!

Complexity Happens

Worldwide, technological breakthroughs occur every few seconds, with hundreds of associated implications, opportunities, and grander challenges. The increasing use of technology in society ensures that you'll always have more with which to contend. In particular, the increase in both the size and the deployment of the Internet means that information is disseminated at much greater speeds and volumes than ever before. Information is power, and people use it to market or sell goods, establish new ventures, or create new ways to gain a leg up on competitors.

Perhaps most onerous for the project manager, as we proceed into the future and as society becomes more complex, is the fact that more-stringent documentation is increasingly required by clients, customers, governmental entities, and even our own organization. The upshot: It's becoming harder to embark on any project without more documentation.

No project goes unscathed. Hiring or firing someone, buying a product, selling something, expanding, merging, casting off—virtually any business function you can name requires more documentation, which contributes to each of us having to handle an increasing amount of administrative-type tasks.

In some organizations, you'll encounter scores of small-to-medium-sized projects with various starting and stopping times throughout the year. Some of these projects are not sufficiently large or complicated to merit the services of a full-time project manager. Thus, individuals might be assigned to manage a project while still maintaining some responsibility for their principal role elsewhere in the organization. Such managers could also find themselves in charge of several small projects whose time frames overlap.

A Tale of Two Offices

In your own career and life, whether you call them projects or not, you probably have already perfected techniques for handling a variety of simultaneous issues or priority items. One key to managing multiple projects effectively is to maintain a clear and separate focus so that when you're working on Project 1, that is the only issue in your mind, and likewise when you are working on Project 2. If you're leading a variety of small projects, mentally separating them has benefits.

My friend and fellow professional speaker Al Walker, from South Carolina, managed two projects a few years ago with aplomb. As a speaker, Al had the continuing task of preparing for his roster of forthcoming speeches. He had to ensure that flights were secured, project materials were delivered to the meeting planner in plenty of time, hotel accommodations were made, and so on. Then, he was elected to the presidency of the National Speakers Association, a post that lasted for one fiscal year.

Al took on the responsibility admirably. He knew that 3,000+ members of the organization were counting on him for effective leadership. To establish a separate focus, Al rearranged his company's offices so that he had a distinct and separate office for his speaking business and another for his role as NSA president. He even had different phone lines installed, plus duplicate support equipment, so that he did not have to shuttle items back and forth between the offices.

As Al walked from office #1 to office #2, in seconds, his focus and attention shifted dramatically.

Extravagance Not Required

Al's approach might sound extravagant. Certainly, you need to have both the space to set up an additional office and the resources to stock both offices adequately for the projects at hand. Yet, many people can accomplish nearly the same. Who doesn't have doubles on some office equipment? Nearly everyone has the room to carve out additional space, perhaps not in a physically distinct office or cubicle, but somewhere within your office, organization, home, vacation home, or other space. You can buy room dividers/noise barriers such as those employed by companies whose workers populate cubicles.

While Al's approach might not be feasible for some, the start-up procedures along with the associated burdens for creating a second office or second work area are offset by the mental clarity and emotional resilience you engender. As you're able to maintain the two work areas, managing two projects becomes more viable. When faced with two major projects of fairly equal weight and complexity, the "two office spaces" approach works as well as any.

Does the above discussion mean that if you're managing three projects it would be advisable to create a third office? No! You can carry any concept too far.

Reporting to More than One Boss at a Time

Related to the issue of managing multiple projects is having to deal with multiple bosses, either on one project or on several projects. The immediate challenge is that either boss is likely to encroach on the schedule you've already devised in pursuit of the assignments doled out by the other boss. Understandably, you could experience a range of anxieties and concerns when having to relay to one boss that plans might have to be delayed because of other activities in which you're involved.

Relations with many bosses, especially in the case of a multiple-boss situation, need to be handled delicately. After all, depending on your organization, bosses could

- Have the power to terminate you without consulting anyone else.
- Conduct performance appraisals that affect your chance to advance in the company.
- Define your job responsibilities. Indeed, the bosses personally might have written your job descriptions.

■ Schedule your work activities. In this respect, your boss might have control over each and every hour that you spend at work, what you work on, how quickly you have to proceed, and which resources you're provided.

■ Have leverage over what benefits you receive.

Reporting to two or more bosses generally is a no-win situation for you. Since you likely lack full control of the situation, you might need to become professionally assertive with your various bosses. In all cases, remain receptive and candid with them. Don't errantly promise everything to everybody and hence create incredible pressure on yourself!

To assert effectively, choose the right time and place, get the listener's attention, pay attention to your tone of voice, state what you want openly and honestly, speak in specifics not generalities, ask questions to foster understanding, seek feedback, and listen to and acknowledge what the other person is saying.

When dealing with each of your multiple bosses:

■ Praise your bosses when they merit praise. Many employees forget that a boss is a person, too, and one who needs positive feedback as much as others do.

■ Assemble your evidence. If you have a point to make, arrive armed with supporting artifacts.

■ Don't dump on your boss. Your boss is not a shoulder to cry on for what went wrong on the project or, for that matter, wrong at home.

■ Pace your communications. Don't overwhelm a boss with more than he or she can comfortably handle. Your project might be only one of many.

■ Take personal responsibility for any department-wide activities or projects in which you're participating.

- Present your situation or problem as succinctly as you can, while maintaining an effective level of interpersonal communication. Don't drone on.

Workaholic for Hire

What about the situation where you're asked to take on too much work, stay too many hours, or handle more responsibility than you're comfortable handling? Here, the ability to assert yourself is certainly valuable.

Suppose you work for a boss who's a borderline workaholic. No, make that a full-fledged workaholic! How can you maintain your job, consistently offer a good performance, maintain sufficient relations, and still have a life? You say *no* without making it sound like *no*:

- *That's something I'd like to tackle, but I don't think it would be in our best interest since I'm already handling XYZ.*
- *I can certainly start on it, but because of the DEF deadline and the XYZ event, I'm certain I won't be able to jump into it headlong until the middle of next month.*
- *If we can park that one for now, I'm sure I can do a good job on it. As you know, I'm handling the HIJ and wouldn't want to proceed unless I could ace the job. If you're eager to have somebody start soon, I wouldn't hesitate to suggest Giselle.*
- *Help me here; I'm not sure what level priority this needs to be in light of the lineup I'm already facing. . . .*

Stand Up for Yourself

Some professionals, fearful that they could lose their job along with their health insurance benefits and other perks, endure various forms of work-related abuse because they lack the ability to assert themselves.

Here is additional, mildly more forceful verbiage, to draw on, depending on circumstances:

- *I'm stretched out on Project A, and if I take this on, I won't be able to give it nearly my best effort. The other tasks that I'm handling will suffer, as well.*
- *Is there anyone else right now who could take on that project? I need to develop a better handle on what I'm already managing.*
- *It's best that I not be put on Project K, if that's okay with you. I've been running long and hard for several months now, and if I don't regain some sense of personal balance, I feel I'm putting my health and my home life at risk.*
- *I wish I could: I've been burning the candle at both ends on Project M, and if I take on more, soon there will be nothing left.*

Asserting Yourself in Dire Situations

Despite your protestations to the contrary, suppose your boss or bosses keep piling on the work and responsibilities. No matter how often and how effective you are at asserting yourself, you're frequently besieged with more assignments and more projects. Here are the two basic options to address the situation. The second option is *not* recommended:

- Push for a compromise situation where you take on some of the new work. Or, take all of it on, but suggest that you'll have to receive additional project resources, such as more people, a bigger budget, or more equipment.

■ Knuckle under and simply take on the added assignments with no additional resources. *Avoid this at all costs!* Instead, compute how many staff hours will be necessary to tackle the added assignment, how much that would cost, and what the overall return will be. And then graciously accept the new project. Likewise, if you need a bigger budget in general, new equipment, or other project resources, figure it out and then ask for it!

■ ■ ■

Managing more than one project at a time, or reporting to two or more bosses, generally is more arduous than managing a single project or reporting to a single boss. Still, you can endure and even prevail. People juggle projects, and bosses, and live to tell about it. With a few of the tips above, you too can become adept.

QUICK RECAP

- Constant advances in technology make us constant multitaskers. This can be a valuable and marketable skill. Managing more than one project at a time is achievable if you can mentally—and maybe also physically—separate your responsibilities.

- Your bosses are human and at least as busy as you are. Respect their time by being concise and organized in your communications, while issuing kudos and praise for their efforts when they are due.

- As a person with a life, sometimes you have to assert your own rights and be assertive in declining additional responsibilities or requesting more support.

- When you're asked to take on more than you can comfortably handle, seek a compromise, or find additional resources, or both.

15

Real-World Project Management Results

In this chapter, you learn why a thorough, initial research phase can pay off handsomely for your project, the difference between squeaking by and excelling, and why open and easy communication is critical to your project's success.

Helping Site Managers to Be More Effective

Marcus works for a large metropolitan construction firm that handles 20 to 40 projects annually, ranging from new-home construction, office buildings, and parking lots to assorted public works projects. Each project is headed by a project foreperson who has various assistants and from 5 to 25 crew members who handle the labor.

Like any business in the construction field, the company has had its ups and downs over the past several years. Regional weather patterns, shrinking municipal budgets, new competition in the marketplace, and a host of other factors keep upper management on their toes.

A good plan, executed by a knowledgeable foreperson with sufficient labor, ideally adds up to overall corporate profitability. It was the owner's belief that as a cadre of highly experienced, well-trained forepersons were established, the profit potential on jobs should improve, if only slightly. Yet, things didn't seem to be working out. One of the biggest challenges, however, was declining profitability per job even as the company matured.

On construction jobs that represented fourth or fifth jobs for a regular client, where the parties involved were relatively seasoned at various processes, profits were down. A thorough audit of the company's practices revealed that the critical issue was high turnover among labor crews.

All other factors—increases in cost of materials, increases in wages, licenses, permits, bonding, insurance, and the dozens of other issues that go hand-in-hand with initiating new constructions—were handled relatively well. In fact, compared to other comparably sized businesses in the field, this particular company was above average in many categories.

Let's Assign It to a Project Manager

Marcus was put in charge of an internal project, authorized directly by the owner. The project mission was to determine why the company was experiencing higher than normal turnover rates among its construction crews, and then to develop a strategy that lowered turnover rates to those of industry and regional standards.

Using the same software that the company employed to manage construction projects, Marcus initiated a project of his own, called "Overturning Turnover"—"OT" for short. Marcus was the solo person on the project; he had no staff. All responsibilities were up to him. What's more, the owner was often lobbying at the state capitol on certain issues, was the chief marketer for the company, and served as the purchasing officer. He had precious little time to spend with Marcus.

Marcus laid out a plan on his own, based on his industry experience. He knew that he would need to speak to each of the forepersons to learn their views, plus several of their assistants as well as the onsite crew chief. Marcus chose to inspect each of the construction sites and then talk face-to-face to the players involved, as opposed to calling, though many of them would have opened up to him over the phone.

Marcus felt certain that the key to successfully completing this project and devising a winning strategy would be found largely at the sites themselves. In the days that followed, he made the rounds, spent time with the key participants he had targeted, and carefully updated his notes.

Armchair Analysis Versus Onsite Observation

After his third visit to a construction site, Marcus felt he had made a breakthrough, but he wanted to confirm his findings and continued to maintain his visitation schedule. Marcus's major observation was that the project forepersons were largely Caucasian, English-speaking males (no surprise to Marcus), whereas over the years, the construction crews comprised an increasing number of immigrants.

The company's far-flung empire extended to several counties and included projects in major urban and suburban areas from which the company recruited its labor. In past years, many Spanish-speaking laborers, a number of whom knew sufficient English to survive, filled the ranks. In fact, among crews with five or more Spanish-speaking laborers, at least one of them spoke fluent English. So, the language barrier did not seem to be a problem, even between the foreperson and a non-English-speaking worker, because a liaison person was always on hand.

As the region began to be inhabited by a more diverse population, construction crews themselves became more diverse. It was not uncommon for a single crew to have several Spanish-speaking workers, as well as natives from Malaysia, Korea, Vietnam, India, Afghanistan, several countries from the Middle East, and various Eastern Europeans, including Albanians, Bulgarians, Greeks, Poles, Czechs, and Romanians.

Many workers also came from Guiana, the Ivory Coast, and Sierra Leone, as well as Somalia, Ethiopia, Uganda, and Kenya. From the western hemisphere, it was not uncommon to have Brazilians, who speak Portuguese; workers from several of the Latin or South American countries; and from French-speaking portions of Canada.

In essence, the company's construction crews on many sites represented a virtual United Nations! When several crew members speaking the same tongue included at least one worker who had decent fluency in English, foreperson-to-crew relations went reasonably well. Often, however, this was not the case. The composition of crew members varied widely from site to site, project to project, and even season to season.

Tower of Babel

Even kind or caring project forepersons could be less effective at their jobs when language barriers diminish effective communication. After delving into the project at length, Marcus realized that slightly increasing turnover rates were due, in part, to the inability of project forepersons to communicate directly with individual crew members.

He reasoned that if countries sometimes ended up going to war with one another over misunderstandings, then it made sense to believe that workers might be departing at higher rates because of their inability to express themselves adequately, be heard and understood, appropriately express frustration or grievances, and, conversely, receive appropriate feedback or even praise.

When he presented his findings to the owner, at first Marcus received a rather cool reception. "It couldn't be that," he was told. "We've had foreign-speaking crew members for years." Marcus persevered and explained that with sophisticated project management software and advancing construction methods, available down time and slack time on many projects were at all-time lows. In other words, construction projects were literally being completed at a quicker pace each year, and the timing, coordination, and precision compared to past operations was a marvel to behold.

Operating at a more efficient pace with little or no slack also meant that there was less overall time for bonding among the workers and conversation in general. Perhaps modern management efficiencies contributed to a "tipping point" in regard to maintaining the human touch.

Slowly but Surely

By and by, the owner acknowledged that Marcus's analysis likely was correct. He then became interested in the strategy that Marcus had devised to "overturn turnover."

As a result of making his rounds and collecting the input of many others, as well as collecting articles from construction industry magazines on this same topic, Marcus had developed a multipart strategy. It was innovative, even if simple and inexpensive. And the owner liked it!

Marcus's plan involved having each foreperson attend a short training program that he himself would personally design. The program would last 90 minutes and only require one handout with printing on both sides of the page. Here is the handout that Marcus devised:

MOTIVATING THE SHORT-TERM CREW MEMBER

Enrique is 19 years old. He came to this country when he was 11, never graduated from high school, and has only a rudimentary grasp of English. Enrique works on one of your crews. He is a good worker, is seldom late, and hardly ever complains. You can feel it, though: He is not going to be at your establishment for long. He will pick up a few dollars and then move on.

Can you increase the job length for workers like Enrique? Indeed, can you motivate someone who, quite bluntly, toils for long hours for little reward? The answer is a resounding "Yes." It will require a little effort and ingenuity on your part; still, Enrique and others in his situation could yet depart on short or no notice. The odds that they will remain with the job longer, however, will increase if you follow some of the guidelines for motivating these employees.

1. *Check Your Attitude*—You need to check your attitude before any motivation program can succeed. As human beings, we broadcast messages all the time. What are you broadcasting to your crews? That they are replaceable? That you are not concerned with their needs?

   It's easy for the foreperson or supervisor who has watched dozens of laborers come and go to develop the view that "It's the nature of the business, so why fight it?" It is that attitude that partially perpetuates the massive turnover in the industry. Resolve that you can take measures to increase the average longevity of low-paid laborers, and your attitude and initiative will make a difference.

2. *An Encouraging Word*—How long would it take you to learn some key phrases in Vietnamese, or the language of

your low-paid laborers? Whether they speak Spanish, Korean, or Farsi, it won't take much time to master some short conversational pleasantries.

Many bookstores are stocked with dictionaries providing various language translations.

Online, you can find key phrases with pronunciation guides in seconds. Even easier, sit down with one of your key crew members. On a piece of paper, jot down the phonetic spelling of phrases such as "How are you today?" and "You're doing a good job."

3. *Unannounced Breaks*—Periodically throughout the day, and especially on challenging days, give your workers unannounced breaks. Augment these mini-vacations by distributing snacks.

The few dollars you spend will pay off in terms of greater productivity that day. These breaks will also enhance longevity among crew members. It pays to offer little perks.

4. *Rotating Leadership*—Rotate leadership among some crews. For instance, on four consecutive days, make sure that crew members each have one day as "foreperson."

For some of your workers, this might represent their first taste of leadership! Rotating leadership is most effective when the crew members are unfamiliar with each other.

5. *Awards System*—Make "contests" short in duration and high on visuals. For example, you could keep a chart on the wall or other visible location indicating who has had the most consecutive days without being absent or tardy. Which crew performances have prompted words of praise from customers? Who has gone above and beyond the call of duty in the last week?

You can easily chart and share these achievements with crew members on duty. People like to see their names on a chart, followed by stars or other performance indicators. The chart could be language proof, for instance. Everyone recognizes their own name in English, and stars or dollar signs can indicate the bonuses you'll offer. After posting the charts, offer simple rewards, which could include cash or more time as a team leader.

6. *Develop Mentors*—Seek leaders among your crew members who can serve as mentors to newly hired staff. This alleviates having to break in each crew member.

Those individuals selected as mentors will be pleased with this special status and will not only assist in achieving smoother operations, but will also help forestall or even eliminate quick departures among new employees.

7. *Use a Checklist*—Here's a checklist to help you determine if you are raising or lowering morale, increasing or decreasing crew members' length of stay, and serving as a leader, not merely as a manager:

- Do I ensure that employees understand how to properly complete a job?
- Have I clearly indicated what results I expect?
- Do I offer adequate and ongoing support?
- Do I cultivate positive relationships?
- Do I show concern for crew members as individuals?
- Have I established appropriate recognition and reward systems?
- Did I learn and dispense encouraging phrases for enhanced communication?

If you practice the above recommendations, you still won't completely eliminate quick turnover or enhance crew motivation. Yet, if you can induce some seasonal crew members to stay on an extra week or encourage them to finish a big job on time, then you have made your job a little easier, and have contributed to the profitability and long-term viability of the company.

After the Handout

Marcus covered the entire program during this session and then requested each foreperson to employ at least one of the measures, with each crew member, at least once per week. With, say, 15 crew members on a project, the foreperson was responsible for one of the following measures per crew member, per week, for a total averaging three such instances a day:

- Offering an encouraging word in the crew member's native tongue
- Giving workers unannounced, on-the-spot breaks
- Rotating leadership among some groups, and so on

Each project manager would then report back to Marcus at the close of each work week so that they could assess progress.

Happily, progress was visible from the *first* day on! Foreign-born crew members perked up immediately when people said a few words or phrases to them in their native language.

After the first week, forepersons reported an increased level of vibrancy, higher morale, and even a higher energy level. At the end of several weeks, the forepersons were convinced that the program was sound.

■ ■ ■

Marcus Scores Big—After several months, as they looked at the data on a project-by-project basis, Marcus and the owner determined that turnover rates were dropping. Workers were staying onboard longer and didn't need to be replaced as often. Project profitability was rising. Both Marcus and the owner certainly felt great about that.

QUICK RECAP
- Even highly qualified, expert professionals are only as adept at managing as they are at communicating effectively with their teams.

- When researching your own internal issues, speak to everyone who might be able to provide insight, face to face if you can.

- Be observant of your environment, and also of *their* environment, to help ensure at the outset that your project is headed in the right direction.

- Meet with your sources on their turf, which prompts them to be more open and candid, and which helps you to see aspects of the project you might have overlooked.

- As much as any other factor, the morale and good motivation among the troops are spurred on by the positive attitude of management.

- Even a menial task can be regarded as worthwhile by a worker, if he or she receives positive reinforcement for a job well done.

16

Learning from Your Experience

In this chapter, you learn how to maintain perspective in your role as project manager, the enduring value of mastering project management software, why it pays to keep your eyes and ears open, and how to be ready for what's next.

Life Is for Learning

Whether you volunteered to lead your current project or were assigned to it, and whether you eagerly anticipate starting work each day or dread it, it's vital to keep your role as project manager in perspective. Managing a project—and managing it well—often leads to managing larger projects; acquiring increasingly valuable, marketable skills; being promoted as a supervisor, manager, or department head; gaining respect and admiration; and earning increases in pay, bonuses, and other perks.

Perhaps you were assigned the role of project manager because no one else was available. Or, someone higher up in your organization believed that you likely could handle the job. Maybe you are being groomed to tackle even greater levels of responsibility.

Any project can be viewed as a stepping-stone along your long-term career path. No project is too inconsequential, too low a priority, or too outside your immediate interest area. Some projects represent large steps and some tiny steps. In each case, you have several opportunities:

- Undoubtedly you will learn things along the way that you can unleash at other times and places in your career. What opportunities, educational or otherwise, might ensue? These opportunities, educational or otherwise, might occur: learning new software, meshing well with diverse groups of people, influencing others (since as a project manager at every point along the way you are selling one thing or another), and gaining a greater appreciation for your organization's processes.
- When you work with a project team, you develop bonds with individuals who have potential future value. Maybe they will work with you on other projects. Perhaps you will be reporting to them on projects. Their skills and interests ultimately might positively affect the direction of your career path.
- Even if you can't *stand* some of your project staff, you can cultivate your ability to manage effectively. At times in your career you'll have to work with less than palatable types. You might as well hone your skills now.
- Working on a project that represents a departure from what you were managing previously exposes

you to new vistas. Perhaps your experience enables you to witness another aspect of your own organization. Conceivably you deal with external elements that represent new and challenging ground for you. Hopefully, you will become more in tune to your own weaknesses as a manager, as a career professional, and as an individual. As such, many a project manager has enrolled in a course or received additional training or sought certification as a result of tackling a challenging project.

■ You step into the batter's box where, potentially, all eyes are focused on you. Taking on a project means that others count on you for specific performance over a specific time interval. The authorizing party and the stakeholders have a vested interest in your progress. Being the object of near-constant scrutiny means that you gain the chance to shine in ways that otherwise might be difficult to muster if you were simply performing routine work as part of the rank and file.

In short, consider the opportunity to manage projects, whether large or small, desirable or undesirable, as the distinct opportunities for professional growth that they invariably represent.

Master the Software

People typically don't learn software unless it is critical to their performance, status, or livelihood. Project management software, discussed in Chapter 11, "Choosing Project Management Software," and Chapter 12, "A Sampling of Popular Programs," is applicable to far more than the project at hand. Whatever software skills you develop on the current project are likely to prove valuable on future projects, both for your organization and for those projects you choose to take on individually.

At home, for instance, you might discover the ability to use what you've learned on the job to accomplish the following:

- Maintain a greater level of control of household expenditures.
- Plot the path that you need to take in order to retire by a desired age.
- Coordinate personal travel plans as never before.
- Help your children to reach their goals in academics, sports, or the arts.
- Manage a household renovation project.

Keep Your Eyes Open

How projects are initiated in your organization—by whom, when, and for what desired result—tells you much about the workings of your organization. Are projects routinely initiated as a result of deadlines or competitive pressures? Do they represent customer service initiatives undertaken by the organization to enhance its overall product or service offerings, even in the absence of immediate pressure to achieve more? Forward-thinking organizations purposely operate according to the latter.

Forward-thinking organizations don't wait for dire circumstances to surface; they proceed in a "managing the beforehand" mode, recognizing that proactive organizations stay in the lead by routinely taking leading, decisive actions.

Whether you're working for an organization that operates in a crisis mode, one with a leading-edge orientation, or one someplace in between, as a result of your observations as a project manager you'll likely encounter other opportunities for your organization.

If you stay alert, the execution of your project in pursuit of the desired outcome inevitably leads to insights worth reporting to your authorizing party and stakeholders. Staying alert could lead to the formulation of new projects which, conveniently, will probably be managed by you! Think of it as a Machiavellian win-win situation where you are selfishly identifying what else you'd like to be managing, which happens to coincide with what benefits your organization.

In this regard, you begin to assume more control over your career path than seemed within your grasp before initiating your current project. Effective project managers often create their own path by identifying one project after another. Such projects help both their organizations and the project managers' own careers.

Along the way, everything that worked well, added to any roadblocks, obstacles, and flat-out failures, becomes useful experience. While you obviously don't seek to incur a series of frustrations on your current project, recognize that what you experience is a "lesson" for another day that can serve to benefit you in one way or another. Then, current ordeals don't need to seem so onerous. You can progress, long term, handling the good along with the bad.

Preparing for the Next Project

Since the effective execution of one project often leads to another one, what are you experiencing and accomplishing along the way to improve your capability and readiness to tackle new projects? For example, are you

- Maintaining a notebook or file on your hard drive of key project insights?
- Denoting the skills and capabilities in detail of the project staffers who contributed to the project in some way?
- Compiling a resource file of books, audiovisual material, software, websites, supporting organizations, and other resources that could be useful on future projects?
- Establishing relationships with vendors, suppliers, consultants, and other outside product and service advisors?
- Cultivating relationships with stakeholders, be they top managers, the authorizing party, clients, customers, other project managers, project team members, department or division heads, plus controllers, accountants, and administrative staff?
- Are you pacing yourself so that if you are requested to leap into something else immediately after completing this project, you will be more or less ready? Maintaining such readiness encompasses taking care of yourself, eating balanced meals, perhaps taking vitamin supplements, getting adequate rest, exercising, practicing stress reduction techniques, and allowing yourself to have a life *during* the course of the project.

In closing, the words of Rudyard Kipling in his classic poem *If* are apropos:

If

by Rudyard Kipling

If you can keep your head when all about you
Are losing theirs and blaming it on you;
If you can trust yourself when all men doubt you,
But make allowance for their doubting too;

If you can wait and not be tired by waiting,
Or, being lied about, don't deal in lies,
Or, being hated, don't give way to hating,
And yet don't look too good, nor talk too wise;

If you can dream—and not make dreams your master;
If you can think—and not make thoughts your aim;
If you can meet with triumph and disaster
And treat those two impostors just the same;

If you can bear to hear the truth you've spoken
Twisted by knaves to make a trap for fools,
Or watch the things you gave your life to broken,
And stoop and build 'em up with worn-out tools;

If you can make one heap of all your winnings
And risk it on one turn of pitch-and-toss,
And lose, and start again at your beginnings
And never breathe a word about your loss;

If you can force your heart and nerve and sinew
To serve your turn long after they are gone,
And so hold on when there is nothing in you
Except the Will which says to them: "Hold on!"

If you can talk with crowds and keep your virtue,
Or walk with kings—nor lose the common touch;
If neither foes nor loving friends can hurt you;
If all men count with you, but none too much;

If you can fill the unforgiving minute
With sixty seconds' worth of distance run—
Yours is the Earth and everything that's in it,
And—which is more—you'll be a Man, my son!

QUICK RECAP

- Effectively managing a project often leads to managing larger projects; being promoted as a supervisor, manager, or department head; and pay increases, bonuses, and other perks.

- Any project holds the potential to become a stepping stone along your long-term career path. Therefore, avoid regarding any project as too inconsequential, too low a priority, or too outside your immediate interest area.

- Effective project managers create their own path by identifying one project after another, which helps both their organizations and the project manager's own career.

- Pace yourself so that if you're requested to jump into something else immediately after completing this project, you will be ready!

Glossary

activity A unit of work usually having a duration, cost, and resource requirement.

activity feed A display of all or the most relevant, useful activity occurring on a website, including user behavior, such as updating, contributing, browsing, and searching.

Agile An approach to management and a way of thinking that focuses on human communication, being flexible in the face of changing situations, and delivering workable, demonstrable results.

Agile Practice Guide Created in partnership with Agile Alliance, this book offers tools, guidelines, and a compilation of Agile approaches to project management, and is geared toward steering "traditional" project managers to a more-Agile approach.

analytical approach Overcoming challenges by reducing them to divisible elements to better comprehend each element and resolve an issue; in contrast to the systems approach.

bottom-up approach A progression from individual elements to the whole.

bottom-up budgeting A financial plan for a defined period of time where participants offer vital input in establishing their own budgets and, collectively, an overall budget.

clocking Summing project team member hours expended on various tasks and subtasks to generate reports that depict actual versus scheduled use of resources.

cloud-based Internet services, applications, or resources available to users on demand from a provider's servers.

collaborative system An organized method in which multiple users can engage in a shared activity, often from remote locations.

contingency plan An alternative course of action in case the originally proposed one encounters significant barriers or roadblocks.

corporate culture The sum total of prevailing practices, methods of operation, beliefs, morals, and widely held notions that perpetuate themselves within an organization and which help to define, as well as limit, the range of behaviors and activities available to members of the culture.

cost benefit analysis A determination of whether to proceed with a proposed solution based on needed monetary, time, and resources versus the desirability of the outcome.

cost control Allocating costs to various project resources, fueled via software, by determining how much resource time and effort will be consumed.

crash time The least amount of time to accomplish a task if unlimited resources are available, such as all the equipment or money a project manager could seek.

crashing Allocating more resources to a task to complete it in less time than originally allotted, potentially enabling the entire project to be completed in less time.

critical path The longest complete path, in duration, of a project. It reveals which sequence of activities has the least amount of slack time.

critical task A single task along a critical path.

culture The lifestyle and prevailing beliefs of a population within a populated unit, such as a community, organization, state, or nation, or within an association, cyber community, or other method of affiliation.

customer portal A web page devised to enhance a user's experience and command of functions that the website is designed to address.

dashboard A software-based control panel for one or more applications or network devices, often used interchangeably with the term *customer portal*.

deliverables Something of value generated by a project management team as scheduled, offered to an authorizing party, reviewing committee, client or constituent, or other stakeholder, in the form of a plan, report, prescript procedure, product, service, or desired outcome.

dependent task A task or subtask that can't be initiated until a predecessor task or several predecessor tasks are completed.

developer application programming interface (API) A set of communication protocols, subroutine definitions, and tools for creating software.

dummy task A link that shows an association or relationship between two otherwise parallel tasks along a CPM network.

embedded capabilities A controlling and operating system with a programmed, dedicated function that performs within a larger system.

environment One's surroundings at work, one's office, surrounding offices, and workplace.

filesharing A system for providing or distributing access to digital media, such as computer programs, documents, or multimedia.

flowchart A quality control tool that records information about process flow.

full path The charted route on a project critical path diagram from the first task to the final outcome.

hand-holding Guidance or support provided during a period of change, learning, or implementation.

holistic The organic or functional relations between the part and the whole.

interfacing The process of connecting with remote staff and project stakeholders, sharing data and information as needed.

jargon Language, expressions, or key terms employed in context by a particular group or industry (which might prove difficult for outsiders to comprehend).

Kanban Method Managing work and the creation of products by balancing demands with available capacity and response to system bottlenecks, emphasizing continual delivery while not overburdening a development team.

lean method A systematic approach to waste minimization without sacrificing productivity.

micro culture A culture within a division, department, branch, or project team, or within an entire corporation itself.

microblogging The practice of offering short, frequent posts representing a mix of blogging and instant messaging to be shared with a targeted audience.

milestone A notable event or juncture in a project that marks the start, or finish, of a significant activity.

Murphy's Law The age-old axiom that if something can go wrong, it *will* go wrong.

network configuration A depiction of tasks and subtasks in a PERT or CPM analysis.

noncritical task A task within a CPM network for which slack time is available.

objective A desired outcome; something worth striving for; the overarching goal of a project; or the reason a project was originally initiated.

over-glut The combination of too much information and communication that can thwart a person's ability to remain focused and be productive.

parallel tasks Two or more tasks that can be undertaken at the same time while not necessarily having the same starting and ending times.

Parkinson's Law The age-old axiom that "Work expands so as to fill the time allotted for its completion."

path A chronological sequence of tasks, each dependent on predecessors; tasks arranged in order, with predecessor tasks preceding dependent tasks.

peer-to-peer collaboration A network where individual computers can transmit information directly to one another, without passing through a centralized server.

PMI professional certification A status conferred by the Project Management Institute based on exacting standards and ongoing research that conveys that a recipient possesses real-world project management capabilities.

politics The relationship of two or more people with one another, including the degree of power and influence that the parties have over one another.

precedence If the completion of one event has priority over another, then that event has precedence over the other.

predecessor task A task that must be completed before another task can commence.

priority queue An element or factor in a situation that is deemed to have status and hence is served or addressed before another element or factor deemed to have lower status.

process The transformation of inputs into outputs through a set of interrelated tasks, steps, or actions performed to attain a particular outcome.

process framework Creating the foundation for a complete software operation, including umbrella activities applicable across the entire software process, by identifying a tiny number of framework activities applicable to all software projects.

process management Aligning operations within an organization to discover, analyze, measure, model, optimize, improve, and automate procedures.

project constraint A critical project element such as money, time, or human resources that often could be in short supply.

project director The individual to whom a project manager reports, who maintains a big-picture focus and not a day-to-day focus on project activities. *Note:* Project directors might have several project managers reporting to them and hence need briefings at specified intervals.

project environment The political, legal, technical, social, economic, and cultural backdrop within which a project team operates.

project lifecycle A multistep process including initiation, planning, execution, and closure, observed by project managers when progressing to project completion. *Note:* Some models include another step, *performance and control,* inserted before "closure."

Project Management Institute The world's largest project management organization with more than 500,000 global members and some 300 local chapters internationally; an authoritative source on project management, offering professional certifications that signify expertise and confer status on recipients.

project management suite A software package that includes strategically designed programs and support tools such as task management, milestones, file sharing, and time-tracking, to aid in successfully managing and competing projects.

project manager An individual with responsibility for overseeing all aspects of the day-to-day activities in pursuit of a project, including coordinating staff, managing the budget, allocating resources, and coordinating efforts to attain a specific, desired result.

project tracking A system for identifying and documenting progress performance for effective review and dissemination to others.

project visualization A graphic representation of quantifiable measures to enhance project members' or stakeholders' understanding of the progress on a project.

real-time The actual time in which something occurs. *Note:* In computing, a degree of computer responsiveness that users sense or experience as sufficiently immediate.

resource load simulators A tool or process that helps forecast resource needs before a project start date and helps gauge if requisite resources and skill levels are available.

return on investment (ROI) The ratio between the net profit and cost of investment resulting from consumption of resources, primarily used to measure the gain or loss on a venture relative to the amount of funds invested.

risk The degree to which a project or portions of one are in jeopardy of not being completed on time, on budget, and at the desired quality level.

schedule A planned, logical sequence of events with start and finish times, detailing resources required.

scheduling tools Project management software, organizers, electronic calendars, time management software, day planners, and other devices that support one's use of time and enhance one's productivity.

scope of work The level of activity and effort necessary—as measured by staff and nonstaff hours, days, resources to be consumed, and funds to be spent—to complete a project and achieve the desired outcome.

scrum An approach to effective team collaboration in which people can address complex or evolving issues, while delivering high-value products or outcomes; a communication tool within an Agile framework and a method for organizing tasks to promote agility.

security protocols A safeguarding operation applying cryptographic protection to ensure the integrity and security of information packets transmitted via a network connection.

servant leadership A leadership philosophy and practice that involves sharing authority, considering the needs of others first, and assisting people to develop their skills and to perform their work optimally.

slack Margin or extra room to accommodate anticipated potential shortfalls in planning.

slack time Time interval when someone has leeway as to when a particular task needs to be completed.

sprints In the Agile framework, doing work in pieces that eventually add up to desired results.

SSL security The standard safeguard technology used to establish an encrypted link between a browser and a web server, ensuring that all transmitted data remains private and intact.

stakeholder Someone who has a vested interest in having a project succeed; stakeholders could include the authorizing party, top management, department and division heads within an organization, other project managers and project management teams, clients, constituents, and parties external to an organization.

subcontract An agreement with an outside vendor for specific services, often to alleviate a project management team of a specific task, tasks, or an entire project.

subtask A slice of a complete task; a divisible unit of a larger task. Usually, a series of completed subtasks leads to the completion of a task.

suitability filters A consistent method for assessing the appropriateness of candidate projects to an Agile development approach and for identifying potential risks.

sync To link operationally.

systems approach A cohesive way to approach problems involving varied and interdependent relationships, standing in contrast to the analytical approach.

task A divisible, definable unit of work related to a project, which might include subtasks.

task dependencies The relationships among tasks which determine the order of activities to be performed.

task histories A software feature that provides information about executed tasks assembled in a relational database for review and analysis.

time line The scheduled start and stop times for a subtask, task, phase, or entire project.

Tinderbox A tool for capturing and visualizing ideas using flexible maps, charts, and flagged terms to more easily visualize intricate qualitative coding projects.

top-down approach A traditional approach to planning, managing, or budgeting that relies on the specifications, and vision, of upper management.

total slack time The cumulative sum of time that various tasks can be delayed without delaying the completion of a project.

trade-offs Options regarding the allocation of scarce resources.

"what-if?" analysis Facilitated by project management software, identifying the immediate impact of altering the order of subtasks, shuffling resources, or changing task dependencies.

work breakdown structure (WBS) Project plans that delineate all the tasks that must be accomplished to successfully complete a project from which scheduling, delegating, and budgeting are derived; a complete depiction of all the tasks necessary to achieve successful project completion.

work statement A detailed description of how a particular task or subtask will be completed, including the specific actions necessary, resources required, and outcome to be achieved.

work-life balance The ability to experience a sense of control and to stay productive and competitive at work while maintaining a happy, healthy home life with sufficient leisure; attaining focus and awareness, despite seemingly endless tasks and activities competing for one's time and attention.

Further Reading

Andersen, Erling. 2008. *Rethinking Project Management*. New York: Pearson.

Archibald, Russell. 2003. *Managing High-Technology Programs and Projects*. New York: John Wiley and Sons.

Barker, Stephen. 2009. *Brilliant Project Management*. Upper Saddle River, NJ: FT Press.

Brown, James. 2014. *The Handbook of Program Management*. New York: McGraw-Hill.

Cleland, David. 1998. *Project Management: Strategic Design and Implementations*. New York: McGraw Hill.

Davidson, Jeff. 2007. *Breathing Space: Living & Working at a Comfortable Pace in a Sped-Up Society*. Scotts Valley, CA: CreateSpace.

———. 2002. *The Complete Guide to Public Speaking*. New York: John Wiley and Sons.

———. 2014. *Dial It Down, Live It Up*. Naperville, IL: Source-books.

———. 2015. *Simpler Living Handbook*. New York: Skyhorse.

Dinsmore, Paul. 1993. *The AMA Handbook of Project Management*. New York: Amacon.

Frame, J. D. 2003. *Managing Projects in Organizations*. San Francisco: Jossey-Bass.

———. 2002. *The New Project Management*. San Francisco: Jossey-Bass.

Frankin, Melanie. 2014. *Agile Change Management: A Practical Framework*. Philadelphia: Kogen Page.

Hallows, Jolyon. 2005. *Information Systems Project Management*. New York: Amacom.

Heagney, Joseph. 2011. *Fundamentals of Project Management*. New York: Amacom.

Kerzner, Harold. 2009. *Project Management: A Systems Approach*. New York: John Wiley and Sons.

Kezsbom, Deborah, et al. 1989. *Dynamic Project Management*. New York: John Wiley and Sons.

Kostner, Jaclyn, Ph.D. 1994. *Knights of the TeleRound Table*. New York: Grand Central.

Larson, Elizabeth, and Richard Larson. 2015. PMI-PBA® *Certification Study Guide*. Philadelphia: Project Management Institute.

Lauren, Benjamin. 2018. *Communicating Project Management*. Abingdon, UK: Routledge.

Levasseur, Robert. 2001. *Breakthrough Business Meetings*. Bloomington, IN: iUniverse.

Lewis, James. 2006. *The Project Manager's Desk Reference*. New York: McGraw-Hill.

Lientz, Bennett, and Kathryn Rea. 2001. *Project Management for the 21st Century*. Philadelphia: Taylor & Francis.

Mackenzie, Kyle. 1998. *Making It Happen: A Non-Technical Guide to Project Management*. New York: John Wiley and Sons.

Meredith, J. R., and Samuel Mantel. 2008. *Project Management*. New York: John Wiley and Sons.

Pinto, Jeffrey. 2015. *Project Management: Achieving Competitive Advantage*. New York: Pearson.

Postman, Neil. 1985. *Amusing Ourselves to Death: Public Discourse in the Age of Television*. New York: Penguin.

Powell, Colin. 2003. *My American Journey*. New York: Ballantine Books.

Project Management Institute. 2018. *A Guide to the Project Management Body of Knowledge*. Philadelphia: PMI.

Schwalbe, Kathy. 2015. *Information Technology Project Management*. Boston: Cengage Learning.

Subramanian, Satish. 2015. *Transforming Business with Program Management*. Boca Raton, FL: Auerbach Publications.

Verzuh, Eric. 2011. *The Fast Forward MBA in Project Management*. New York: John Wiley and Sons.

Weiss, Joseph, and Robert Wysocki. 1992. *5-Phase Project Management*. Boston, MA: Perseus.

Williams, Paul. 1996. *Getting a Project Done on Time*. New York: Amacom.

Acknowledgments

I would like to acknowledge the fine folks at Berrett-Koehler Publishers for initiating such a nifty series, including, in alphabetical order, María Jesús Aguiló, Director of Subsidiary Rights; Leslie Crandell, Senior Sales Manager; Michael Crowley, Associate Director of Sales and Marketing; Sean Davis, Operations Manager; Matt Fagaly, Social Media Strategist; Sohayla Farman, Production Assistant; Maren Fox, Digital Marketing Specialist; Kristen Frantz, Vice President of Sales and Marketing; Lesley Iura, Director of Professional Publishing; Arielle Kesweder, Associate Director of Operations; Catherine Lengronne, Associate Director, Subsidiary Rights; Zoe Mackey, Director of Digital Marketing; David Marshall, Vice President, Editorial and Digital; Shabnam Banerjee-McFarland, Sales and Marketing Strategist; Liz McKellar, Trade and International Sales Specialist; Sarah Modlin, Editorial Assistant; Kate Piersanti, Copyright Editor; Steven Piersanti, President and Publisher; Katie Sheehan, Senior Communications Manager; Johanna Vondeling, Vice President International Sales and Business Development; Edward Wade, Director, Design and Production; Lasell Whipple, Design Director; and Chloe Wong, Sales and Marketing Assistant.

Much thanks as well to JodieAnne Sclafani and Susan Baker of Westchester Publishing Services; and especially to my acquisition and managing editor, Charlotte Ashlock, Executive Editor. Much thanks as well to the expert reviewers, Tammy Stark, Pamela Gordon, and Ken Fracaro, and to my student proofreaders, Aidan Mangan and Ben Moretz.

Index

About the Author

Jeff Davidson served nine years as a full-time management consultant for firms in Connecticut and Washington, D.C. At age 30, he obtained the Certified Management Consultant designation (CMC) as bestowed by the Institute of Management Consultants, the world's premier certifying  organization for management consultants. Jeff headed scores of projects involving marketing and management, as well as others in finance, production, light manufacturing, wholesaling, and professional services, directing teams ranging from two to eight people with budgetary responsibilities up to $490,000.

Since his years in management consulting, Jeff has managed another type of project—writing books. He is the author of 68 books and 32 ghostwritten books, as well as many booklets, guides, and special reports. These publication projects range from one month to 18 months in duration, involving numerous researchers, editors, and subject matter experts. Project tasks include interviewing, researching, copyediting, obtaining permissions, and assisting publishers with marketing and promotion.

Jeff's books have been selected by book clubs 41 times; translated into 19 languages, including Arabic, Chinese, Finnish Japanese, Malay, Spanish, Turkish, and Russian; and sold in foreign countries or territories a total of 151 times. His books are the basis for several audio albums, videos, and online training programs. They have been featured in 68 of the top 75 American newspapers and, in two instances, advertised in *Time* magazine and the *Wall Street Journal*.

On the web at www.BreathingSpace.com, Jeff holds the registered trademark as "The Work-Life Balance Expert."® He currently speaks at conventions and conferences to organizations and groups that seek to enhance productivity by improving the work-life balance of their people. Jeff has spoken to Fortune 50 companies such as IBM, Cardinal Health Group, and Lockheed; and to American Express, National Office Furniture, Wells Fargo, and Westinghouse; and in total has spoken professionally more than 900 times.

Jeff's current book titles include *Simpler Living; Breathing Space;* and *Perfect Timing.* He has been interviewed 19 times in the aggregate by the *Washington Post, Los Angeles Times, Chicago Tribune, Christian Science Monitor, New York Times,* and *USA Today.*

Jeff is also a columnist for 15 publications, among them *Accounting Web, ATD Career Development, Business Performance, Human Resources, Inside Business, Meeting Professional, Physician's Practice, Practical Lawyer, Real Estate Professional,* and *Smart Meetings.*

Berrett–Koehler
Publishers

Berrett-Koehler is an independent publisher dedicated to an ambitious mission: *Connecting people and ideas to create a world that works for all.*

Our publications span many formats, including print, digital, audio, and video. We also offer online resources, training, and gatherings. And we will continue expanding our products and services to advance our mission.

We believe that the solutions to the world's problems will come from all of us, working at all levels: in our society, in our organizations, and in our own lives. Our publications and resources offer pathways to creating a more just, equitable, and sustainable society. They help people make their organizations more humane, democratic, diverse, and effective (and we don't think there's any contradiction there). And they guide people in creating positive change in their own lives and aligning their personal practices with their aspirations for a better world.

And we strive to practice what we preach through what we call "The BK Way." At the core of this approach is *stewardship*, a deep sense of responsibility to administer the company for the benefit of all of our stakeholder groups, including authors, customers, employees, investors, service providers, sales partners, and the communities and environment around us. Everything we do is built around stewardship and our other core values of *quality, partnership, inclusion,* and *sustainability.*

This is why Berrett-Koehler is the first book publishing company to be both a B Corporation (a rigorous certification) and a benefit corporation (a for-profit legal status), which together require us to adhere to the highest standards for corporate, social, and environmental performance. And it is why we have instituted many pioneering practices (which you can learn about at www.bkconnection.com), including the Berrett-Koehler Constitution, the Bill of Rights and Responsibilities for BK Authors, and our unique Author Days.

We are grateful to our readers, authors, and other friends who are supporting our mission. We ask you to share with us examples of how BK publications and resources are making a difference in your lives, organizations, and communities at www.bkconnection.com/impact.

Dear reader,

Thank you for picking up this book and welcome to the worldwide BK community! You're joining a special group of people who have come together to create positive change in their lives, organizations, and communities.

What's BK all about?

Our mission is to connect people and ideas to create a world that works for all.

Why? Our communities, organizations, and lives get bogged down by old paradigms of self-interest, exclusion, hierarchy, and privilege. But we believe that can change. That's why we seek the leading experts on these challenges—and share their actionable ideas with you.

A welcome gift

To help you get started, we'd like to offer you a **free copy** of one of our bestselling ebooks:

www.bkconnection.com/welcome

When you claim your **free ebook**, you'll also be subscribed to our blog.

Our freshest insights

Access the best new tools and ideas for leaders at all levels on our blog at ideas.bkconnection.com.

Sincerely,

Your friends at Berrett-Koehler